◄ THE BEST OF

D0846395

J E R E M I A H

People

Humorous Sketches & Performance Tips from America's Leading Christian Repertory Group

Compiled and Edited by

JIM CUSTER and BOB HOOSE

MERIWETHER PUBLISHING LTD.
Colorado Springs, Colorado

Meriwether Publishing Ltd., Publisher
P.O. Box 7710
Colorado Springs, CO 80933

Editor: Rhonda Wray
Typesetting: Cheryl Tuder, Sharon Garlock and Beth Tallakson
Cover design: Beth Tallakson
Cover photo: Wayne Epperson

© Copyright MCMXCI Continental Ministries
Printed in the United States of America
First Edition

Library of Congress Cataloging-in-Publication Data

Custer, Jim, 1951 –
    The best of the Jeremiah people : humorous sketches and performance tips from America's leading Christian repertory group / by Jim Custer & Bob Hoose. — 1st ed.
        p.   cm.
    ISBN 0-916260-81-X : $14.95
    1. Christian drama, American.   I. Hoose, Bob, 1956– .
II. Title.
PS3553.U78B37 1991
812.54080382—dc20   91–34195
                                                  CIP

*We dedicate this book
to **The Jeremiah People** who have been
on the cutting edge of Christian theatre
for over twenty years.*

TABLE OF CONTENTS

PREFACE

WHAT IS A CUSTER HOUSE?

While traveling across the United States on one of our weekend trips, a young boy looked at the trunks that carry our props and asked to his mother, "Mom, what is a Custer House?" You see, our name was stenciled across the back — Custer/Hoose. Yes indeed, folks, we've been called a little of everything: Turner and Hooch, Custard and Hoosie, Bob and Hooch, and a few others that we dare not put in print.

Basically we're a couple of middle-aged men traveling across the country telling churches — YOU CAN DO IT! You can start and maintain a drama ministry, no matter what your church size or resources. Not only that — it can be enormously effective.

Like the little boy who looked at our trunks and asked, "What is a Custer House?", a lot of people look at us and say, "What is drama — and why bring it into church?"

We may be biased, but we feel drama is **the** most powerful tool of communication available today. We are living in a very visual society. People watch on the average of 40 hours of television per week. Now, we don't want to develop or encourage more "couch potatoes," but there is no getting around the fact that we are a society whose main form of communication is through visual arts.

This visual connection is the reason Christian drama is enjoying unprecedented popularity. You can "reach the masses" in a way that they'll respond to enthusiastically. We hope this book enables you to develop your on-stage talents, and also to reach people as you entertain them. You are fortunate to have a built-in audience ready to see and hear what you have to say. Let's get started. Your church is waiting to applaud you!

INTRODUCTION

"*Actors in church?* You gotta be kidding! We're conducting a worship service — not a matinee!"

Twenty years ago, this described the feeling of many pastors and church leaders about Christian drama. Oh, a few Christian drama groups existed back in 1970, but they were primarily for evangelizing those outside the church.

But Cam Floria, president of Continental Ministries, had a new idea in mind. He felt that drama had the potential to be a delightfully different, but influential, ministry. He wanted to organize a group that would perform short sketches and music which would speak specifically to Christians about their relationship with Christ. This bold new idea became a reality when, in 1971, **Jeremiah People** was formed in Woodland Hills, California. That fall, the group went on their first tour, and they have been on the road ever since. (The group is currently based in Denver.)

The name **"Jeremiah People"** came from Jeremiah, the young prophet who was often quoted by Christ. And the similarities extend beyond the name. Jeremiah spoke to the Jewish people about repentance and turning back to God. Likewise, **Jeremiah People's** "mission" has always been to spark renewal — to prod Christians to examine their priorities and deepen their relationship to Christ. Because Jeremiah was young, **Jeremiah People** is composed of young people. Jeremiah made his messages more real to the people by using analogies they could relate to — such as God as the Potter and we, the clay. **Jeremiah People** also uses illustrations to communicate visually through drama.

Group members are selected through auditions, both after performances of the **Jeremiah People** and the Continental Singers, and by resumes and audition tapes sent through the mail. A (mostly) new group, varying from seven to eleven members, is chosen each year.

Now you know how **Jeremiah People** came to be. Who are we now? Several words and phrases come to mind:

Unique. The ministry of the **Jeremiah People** differs in approach from other drama groups. But it hasn't always been easy to find our place. Back in the early Seventies, we were considered a Contemporary Christian music group. But that label didn't exactly fit because we did a *lot* of sketches and a little music. Record companies didn't know what to do with us — they didn't know whether to put the sketches on the album or just the music. It was confusing at the time, but we're glad we kept our identity and didn't compromise our trademark method.

Challenging the Church. We've earned the right to be heard by the church from consistently integrating our original mission of what it is to be a Christian in our drama. We've never shied away from controversial subjects, but we try to approach them in an understanding manner — often with humor. We try to stretch the church — to urge people to look at Christian truths in new ways through drama. We really believe acting is a powerful way of communicating.

Facing Conflict. In our **Jeremiah People** travels, we observe many different problems within the church. If these problems keep resurfacing in church after church, we'll find a way to work them into our material. The failure of Christian drama has been the reluctance to really explore conflict, and yet conflict is at the heart of all good drama. It keeps the audience interested. The minute you resolve conflict is the minute you start to lose your audience.

Progressive. **Jeremiah People** has been "ahead of its time." We've progressed from doing mainly sketches to our current Broadway-type show. But churches interested in drama are just now starting to get enthused about sketches. They're about twenty years behind! For so many years, churches liked drama but, beyond the annual kiddie Christmas pageant, they didn't want it in their services. Now they can't get enough of it. We've been pleased to see that drama is finally recognized as an important part of worship.

Looking Ahead. Where are we headed? We'll continue to experiment; to offer our material in fresh and innovative ways.

Lately we've put on our dancing shoes! The church hasn't been too gung ho on dancing . . . with the exception of some liturgical dancing now and then. **Jeremiah People** has introduced tap and jazz — not to distract, but to add *impact* to the program in a creative way. We'll strive to reach new heights — personally and professionally. And most importantly, we'll continue to be the voice the church needs to hear.

WHY A DRAMA MINISTRY?

Good question. First of all, we believe drama can be used in worship. How, you ask? By introducing the sermon topic. A short three to five minute sketch can put "visual feet" to the topic on which the pastor is prepared to speak. When we were children, our Sunday school teacher used to tell Bible stories and illustrate them with a flannel graph. We were able to "see" the characters, and they came alive to us. Drama, used to introduce or illustrate the sermon, can do the same thing. It can help us identify visually and emotionally with the sermon topic.

Secondly, drama is a great way to expand people's opportunity for ministry. A drama ministry can involve many individuals. We would venture to say that there are people in your congregation who can't sing but they can act, direct, sew, build, write, or technically create any special effects. All of these people can be involved in a drama ministry — they just need the opportunity.

Thirdly, a good drama ministry can bring people together. Nothing is more encouraging than seeing people of all ages working and relating together. We encourage you to open up your drama ministry to the whole church.

Fourthly, a drama ministry can be pure fun! When we say "pure fun," we mean for everyone — not just the participants, but for the observer as well. Good comedy and drama disarms people and opens them up to be taught in a fun way. The longevity of the **Jeremiah People** can attest to that!

When the group began, contemporary drama was virtually nonexistent in the church. Some church leaders said, "It'll never fly," but **Jeremiah People** has been touring now for 21 years, encouraging and teaching Christians with drama and music throughout North America and Great Britain. By God's grace, you can have that same impact right there in your local church.

In the pages that follow, we'll give you some practical, "how to" tips to take the mystique out of blocking, lighting and sound (even on a budget!), theatre games, and other fundamentals. Then you'll find 25 opportunities to practice your newfound knowledge. We're sharing both old favorites and some newer scripts, but all the sketches included in Part Two have been successfully performed by the **Jeremiah People** for audiences nationwide. They are production tested and ready for performance.

We've sufficiently "set the stage," so to speak. Now it's time to cover the basics. Drama is waiting in the wings. Bring it on!

PART ONE

Production Techniques

GETTING STARTED

Skip this section . . . that is, if you have a wealth of church theatre experience, because this section will probably only re-emphasize what you've already discovered yourself. But, if you're only beginning, and maybe a little unsure of your theatrical bearings, then hang in there! Instead of just throwing you a few sketches and saying "OK, do it," we thought we'd include some quick ideas that might help smooth out some of those lines in your troubled brow.

Maybe your church leadership has said, "We'd love to see a drama ministry in our church," or, "Well, perhaps it could be useful . . . let's give it a try." Or they might say, "All right, stop bugging me. You can do it, but only one Sunday, and then we'll see what the congregation's reaction is." Whatever your situation, you need to get started, so . . . *What do you do?*

The first step is to decide what your goals are for the ministry of drama. What does the church want? Will your drama be primarily an evangelistic outreach, discussion starter, youth program, visual illustration for the sermon topic, general worship tool, etc.? Your goals definition can include one or more of the above, but it's important to define. Drama, like any ministry, needs to have a focus and accomplish a purpose.

Another smart step is to know who you should report to. If you are not on staff, then determine who can give you feedback or sermon topic ideas. You need to keep in touch with the pulse of the church, and believe me, the staff members are the first people who'll know if something would cause a "congregational heart attack."

ORGANIZING

The next step is to put feet to some of your ideas and get a group together. What's that, you say? You've wanted to do some sketches but didn't want to have a group meeting on a regular basis? Well, that's fine, but if you want to see your actors improve, your sketches become more believable, and your church accept this as a viable ministry, then we believe a regular weekly meeting is essential. To begin with, announce a first meeting place and time in the bulletin and/or from the pulpit. Invite anyone who might be interested in drama to attend. When the masses show up, hand them two things:

1. A questionnaire (see sample #1, page 7) where they can list all their interests and vital statistics, and an . . .

2. "Expectations and Explanations" sheet (see sample #2, page 9). The E and E sheet should simply list the goals of the group and also your expectations for the individuals in the group. When everyone understands what is required of them (and then conforms to that), rehearsals and performances run *much* smoother. For example, your sheet could stress that they be committed attendees, since anything done should be done to excellence, and excellence is attained only through regular hard work.

The first meeting will also serve as a great place to decide upon a regular night and time that fits everyone's schedule.

All right, now you've got some excited people who want to show up on a weekly basis and work hard. *So what's next?*

REHEARSALS

Weekly rehearsals need to be fun and challenging. An important way to accomplish this is to keep everyone involved. Rehearsals need to be flexible, yet retain some structure. We suggest the following: Start with prayer, unwind with a relaxation exercise, warm up with at least one theatre game, and then rehearse the sketches that are coming up on the church schedule. Two hours is usually a sufficient amount of time to include all this activity. Rehearsing certainly isn't as exciting as being on stage, but the nitty gritty work of practicing is absolutely essential to produce good, confident drama.

A SIDE-NOTE FROM JIM ON THE "C" WORD...
COOPERATION

The regularity of weekly rehearsals is guaranteed to produce friendship within the group. We wouldn't trade our days in **Jeremiah People** for anything. Relationships were established in the early days of the group that continue even today, nurtured by the closeness of rehearsals. Ah, memories . . . like the time in the middle of a performance when one actor was supposed to shake hands with another. This other guy had previously coated his hand with Vaseline. The moment of contact was not a pleasant experience! It was difficult for the show to go on after that because of all the barely suppressed laughter. (Children, don't try this at home!)

Unfortunately, this same familiarity also has the potential to create conflicts. Our group has had conflicts, sure, but friendships didn't dissolve. One key to the success of **Jeremiah People** is limiting rehearsal to two hours a day. We'd say 98% of a successful road tour is how the participants get along. Even if your group decides to "stay put," we're sure you'll find that harmony within the group makes for honest, enthusiastic performances.

One thing I stressed as leader of the group (and this approach is still being used), is honesty, confrontation and commitment to working out the big conflicts, since they usually don't just disappear! Sometimes this is hard to do — a lot of us would rather try to block out problems. On the road there are no options. You have to learn to understand others and get along. When you're not certain what someone thinks of you, problems, either real or imagined, can interfere. If you work on building an atmosphere of unconditional love and acceptance, relationships thrive. When irritations occur, they are easier to deal with because each group member has the reassurance that "no matter what happens, these people care about me."

We tend not to get offended. We tend to let minor irritations roll off our back so they don't have a chance to develop into heavy duty conflicts. Don't let the little things blow out of proportion. We encourage you to either "oh well" it or deal with it.

SAMPLE #1

Date _____

NAME _____

ADDRESS _____

_____

HOME PHONE _____ WORK PHONE _____

AGE _____

Which is the best number to reach you? ☐ Home ☐ Work

What is the best time to reach you? _____ ☐ am ☐ pm

Areas of Interest:

☐ Acting
    ☐ Stage   ☐ Video, Film

☐ Directing
    ☐ Stage   ☐ Video, Film

☐ Scriptwriting

☐ Technical
    ☐ Sound   ☐ Lights   ☐ Camera

☐ Stage Management

☐ Sets
    ☐ Design   ☐ Construction

☐ Stagehand

☐ Stage Props

☐ Costumes
    ☐ Coordination   ☐ Design

☐ Make-Up

☐ Management (Production/Administrative)

☐ Promotion

☐ Catering

☐ Other _____

_____

SAMPLE #2
EXPECTATIONS AND EXPLANATIONS

This drama group is created to:

1. Minister to _____ (your church) and related outreaches through the use of drama, comedy, media, and other art forms, and . . .

2. To nurture and develop the spiritual and creative elements of our members through ministry, various productions, in-group rehearsals, exercises, classes, and experiences.

Our membership consists of those who are in high school or older.

Rehearsals are scheduled for every Tuesday evening from 7:00 to 9:00 pm (insert your own specifics), though additional rehearsals might be necessary for certain projects. Rehearsals are mandatory, with the exception of serious illness or death in the family. As a matter of conscience, we expect that you will always make rehearsals a priority.

Rehearsals will include preparation for upcoming productions, classes, and practical experience through the performing of scenes, improvisations, and related exercises within the group.

Where applicable, we will often require members to prepare themselves for rehearsals and productions through outside memorization of lines, scenes, etc.

In the event of serious illness or death, please give appropriate notice. (Ten minutes before rehearsal is to begin is not appropriate notice, unless the death took place one minute before that.) Otherwise, *be on time.*

While dress and appearance for productions will be dictated by the sketches performed, dress and appearance for rehearsals will be relaxed and informal, though we ask that all attire be sensitive and conducive to good Christian conscience.

Scripts and playbooks, unless specifically purchased by the individual, are the property of the church. We ask that all be returned upon completion of a project. It is also important that scripts, playbooks, and related material be brought to every rehearsal. It is also wise to bring a yellow highlighter, pencil, pen, and notepad.

All egos should be checked at the door. This is a ministry striving to match servanthood and sacrifice with talent. "Star complexes," "prima donnas," "Madonnas," "poor temperaments," and other such attitudes will not be tolerated. Scripture to support this policy will often be made available, whether you like it or not.

It is our sincere desire to nurture a family atmosphere . . . one that will not only explore a talent, but meet with the needs of the hearts behind that talent.

We want you to join our family, grow to understand and appreciate the uniqueness of a ministry such as this, grow to enjoy your God-given abilities, know the satisfaction of excellence in performance or behind-the-scenes work, and feel personal joy as others are affected for Jesus Christ because of your participation.

Inasmuch as your spiritual life will ultimately affect the entire group, we *strongly* suggest that you commit yourself to regular Sunday morning church attendance, daily Bible study and daily personal prayer time.

ACTING EXERCISES AND GAMES

RELAXING

The object of a relaxing exercise is to produce a "clean slate" in your actors. Nothing inhibits acting like tension. Here are some easy exercises to get rid of "the Big T."

Have your actors lie on their backs. They shouldn't be touching anyone or crossing their arms or legs. Now, ask them to close their eyes. Slowly take them through the different areas of the body, having them visualize relaxing each area. Start with the forehead and progress to the feet. At different times in the exercise, have them take a deep breath and exhale through their vocal cords, producing a nice, loud sigh. Don't be surprised if they giggle. Laughing is a way of relaxing, too. At the end of the exercise, you should be able to walk around and pick up their arm or leg and find it free of tension. Now, have them sit up slowly . . . keeping that relaxed feeling.

A second exercise is called the "Rag Doll." Give your actors plenty of space so they can move about without touching anyone. From the waist up, have them pretend to be a Rag Doll . . . free from bones or muscles. Now, have them swing their arms and move their head. Make sure they don't lock knees but have them slightly bent for more mobility.

Another exercise is called the "Melting Ice-Cream Cone." Begin with your actors standing straight up. Have them visualize being an ice-cream cone. As you describe the heat of the day, they should begin to melt until they are puddles of ice-cream on the warm pavement. At the completion of the exercise, have them slowly sit up . . . keeping themselves relaxed.

Now all the actors are refreshed and ready to work. It's time to stretch their "acting muscles."

ACTING MUSCLES

That's right. There are four basic "muscles" that we tend to abandon once we cross over into the land of "Grown Up." These muscles are essential for good dramatic, creative, and communicative skills.

1. *Observation*: So many creative ideas for characters and relationships come from the world around us. Although we live in a very visual society, we very rarely see the things we look at.

2. *Memory*: What actor worth his salt fails to memorize his script? However, in today's rush-rush world, memorizing your own telephone number can be a monumental task.

3. *Imagination*: Without a doubt, this is the most important acting muscle we possess. Imagination can make a tree into a castle, and your pet terrier into a fire-breathing dragon. However, when we lose our imagination, we're stuck with a withered oak and an old mutt.

4. *Concentration*: If we combine the three muscles listed above, we can create something wonderful that can then be cemented in place by concentration. However, today's television has given us a sixty-second attention span.

So what's to do? We need to give these flabby muscles some exercises with theatre games.

THEATRE GAMES

A theatre game is a non-threatening, fun way of teaching and helping people to be better actors. They can be as simple or complicated as your actors can handle. Every theatre game will have two basic goals:

1. To exercise "acting muscles," *i.e.* observation, memory, imagination and concentration; and

2. To establish a community atmosphere in which everyone works together, supports one another, and creativity abounds.

Sound complicated? Nah! Let's start with some simple ones.

SIMPLE GAMES FOR BEGINNERS

1. The Invisible Ball

Ask your actors to stand side by side in a circle. Now show them an invisible ball. While "holding" it in your hands, stress to them that as they pass this magic ball slowly around the circle, they should feel its shape, size, weight, and texture. Now, pass the "ball." As each player takes the ball, ask them questions about its size and shape . . . motivate them to work together and imagine what the player next to them is handing them. After one pass around the circle, you can try it again, only this time the ball can change size and/or weight at your command. Again, they need to work at slowly passing the ball and sensing its new dimensions as you verbally change its properties.

As simple as this game may seem, it not only works all four acting muscles but it also teaches your group to break down the walls we tend to hold around ourselves and begin to work together. This is a great place to start.

2. Mirror Image

Here's a fun game that has been around a long time. Have your group break up into pairs. Have them decide who is player A and who is player B. While looking directly into each other's eyes, they should use their peripheral vision to see all of their partner's movements. Player A starts slowly moving a part of his body and player B must mirror the exact movements. After a few minutes you call out for them to switch, so that B now leads and A follows without a break in the movement. Be sure you remind them to keep the movements slow and fluid.

This exercise really helps with the concentration muscle. It's also very difficult to remain shy while staring into someone's eyes. This is a great ice breaker.

3. Change Three Things

Now, while everyone is still paired up, let's try an easy observation exercise. Give the group 30 seconds to observe their partner. After the alotted time, have the players turn their back to their partner and change three things about the way they look (*i.e.* switch a watch from left to right wrist, take off their earrings, unbutton a button).

Each player should be as creative and subtle as possible to challenge his partner's powers of observation. When everyone is finished with their changes, have them turn around and guess each other's adjustments. This is a good game to prove that we aren't as observant as we like to believe.

OK, so the easy ones are a breeze. Let's keep going. As your actors get used to each other and the way the theatre games work, you can work at creating games that are a bit more demanding. We like to challenge our actors to start thinking on several different levels because most people tend to use multi-level thought processes while acting, even if they're not aware of it. For example, when you're acting, not only are you trying to remember your own lines, but you're also listening and responding to the other characters. Along with that, you are listening to the audience reaction. If someone drops a line or a chair collapses, you should be ready for that, too. Let's try some multi-level games.

MULTI-LEVEL GAMES

1. Three Way Conversation

One group player stands facing forward. Two other players stand on either side of the first player and face him. The players on either side will choose a topic and engage the middle player in conversation as if the other "side" player did not exist. The object of the game is to have the middle player converse with both sides while staying involved with both conversations and excluding no one. Remember that the players on either side converse only with the player in the middle. Did you get that straight? This is a great concentration exercise.

2. Three Different Ages

Teaching young actors to use their imagination and be aware

of their environment is not an easy task, but here's a fun exercise that will definitely develop those muscles. Choose a player and tell him to enter the room as a five-year-old. As he enters, he must take off his coat, drink a glass of water, call for his mother, and exit. Now have him repeat the exercise as an 8, 12, and 18-year-old. It's a challenge, but definitely one that stretches the imagination.

3. Emotional Living Room

This one is basically an improvisation with a twist. Start by choosing two or three players. As with any improvisation, you need to set up some groundwork, *i.e.*:

1. Establish a locale (in this case an apartment would work best).

2. Establish a relationship between the characters (Husband/wife, brothers, boyfriend/girlfriend).

3. Establish a conflict that the players will act out. (Husband just sold the house on the spur of the moment and needs to break the news to his wife while she has just bought new furnishings at a no return bargain sale.)

Now you would think that this would be enough to keep the players challenged, right? Sure, but let's add another level of thought. We'll divide the playing area into three parts and require the players to display an emotional response when they're standing in each area. For example, we have an apartment with kitchen area, living area with a couch, and a study area with a chair, small table, and phone. The player must exhibit anger when in the kitchen, intense joy when in the living area, and paranoia when in the study area. The players can stand in any area they wish (player A could be in the kitchen exhibiting anger while player B is in the living area exhibiting joy). The players must continue to relate to each other while justifying their emotional responses. The exercise ends when both players have been in all three areas. Now if this one doesn't get the players thinking on different levels while exercising all their acting muscles . . . I don't know what will.

STAGING YOUR SKETCH

SETS AND PROPS

There are two basic ways to approach staging your sketch. One is the minimalist approach, the other is with full sets and props. Both can be effective.

Let's take the minimalist approach first. The object of this is to reduce your workload (*i.e.* having to find costumes, extensive props, or sets) and to stretch your audience's imagination. With this approach, you rely on your actors. You should use very few props or costumes and absolutely no sets. The goal is to just give the impression of what you want to convey. For example, if the scene takes place in a living room, then use two or three folding chairs side by side to represent a couch, and that's it. The object is to keep it simple.

The second approach is to use full sets. We would only recommend doing this if you have a weekly series of sketches in the same location (bus station, beauty salon). This approach will cut down on your work load, yet give your sketches a nice, finished effect. A word of caution: make sure your sets are sturdily built. **Jeremiah People** has had sets fall down right in the middle of the show before, and take it from us — nothing "breaks the mood" more than the unexpected crash landing of a section of the living room wall! Whatever you do, *remember*, the actor is the most important part of the production. If the actor understands his/her part and executes it correctly, he/she can make the audience believe whatever he/she wants.

BLOCKING

When you mention "blocking" to people, you get two responses . . . "Huh?" and "Oh, that's my weakest area. I don't know what to do."

Actually, blocking isn't that difficult. Now remembering it from rehearsal to rehearsal could be a problem. So, *write it down!*

Your actors should also write it down. As you move your actors from place to place on the stage, jot it down in the margins of your script.

The three rules of blocking are:

1. Create an interesting picture
2. Balance the stage
3. Give your actors motivation for moving.

Let's look at each one of these rules.

CREATE A PICTURE

First, good blocking creates an interesting picture. Every scene you direct must be interesting to watch. Are your actors in a straight line? If so, is that interesting, or would it be better to stagger them? A nice rule of thumb is to avoid working in straight lines (unless you're the Rockettes at Radio City Music Hall) but instead, work in triangles. It's much more interesting to watch.

CREATE BALANCE

Secondly, balance the stage. OK, use your imagination. Pretend there is a fulcrum directly in the center of the stage. As you stand back and observe the stage, does it look balanced? Do you have three people bunched together on one side of the stage? If so, by stepping back and looking at the overall picture, you can see that if you moved two more cast members to the other side, the stage would look balanced. What about that crowd scene? Your principle actor is getting lost in all the people . . . what do you do? One of the easiest things to do to solve the problem is to elevate him/her. This immediately draws the audience's attention and makes him/her the prominent person on stage.

CREATE MOTIVATION

Thirdly, give your actors a motivation for moving or being

where they are. Traveling across the country as we do, many times we find ourselves in colleges. On one recent trip, we were asked by the director of a college production of *Carousel* to observe their rehearsal. In one dramatic scene, the heroine was mourning the loss of her one true love. A friend was standing on one side of the stage watching. It soon became apparent to us that the friend had no motivation for being there. She didn't know what to do, what to feel. She continued to stand there until it was time for her to say her line, then she immediately clicked into character. As observers, we found this distracting. It would have potentially ruined the scene. To solve the problem, we gave her a reason for being where she was. The next runthrough, she was intimately a part of the scene, not just a piece of furniture. The same principle should be applied to holiday productions. Many times you have people on stage as a part of the town or village. Most of these people do not have lines, yet you must make sure they understand why they are there and what they are doing. It will only help your production to be more believable. Actions must be minimal and make sense. Less is more, and understanding is everything.

LIGHTING AND SOUND

As we travel across the country doing our seminars, people are always asking us about lights and sound. Are they important? Do they have to cost an arm and a leg? The answer to these question are . . . yes, they are important (but not as important as one might think), and no, they don't have to cost you an arm and a leg.

If you have a little extra money in your budget, spend it on lights. You'd be amazed at what a little theatrical lighting can do. With a blue wash using a Par 56 light and a blue gel (approximate cost $120), it can be evening. With an amber glow using a Fresnel light fixture and an amber gel (approximate cost $100), it can be sunrise. It doesn't take much to go a long way.

The other crucial thing about lighting is it can add a period to the end of your scene. When the lights go out, people know it's the end of the scene. There were times with **Jeremiah People** when something would go wrong with our lighting system. You can't travel 50,000 miles a year doing six concerts a week without some technical problems. Whether or not we could get the system up, we always made sure we got at least one light operating. I'll never forget seeing our sound/lighting tech with his hands on the sound board ready to kill the mikes at the end of the scene and an electrical cord in his teeth ready to unplug the one light we had focused on the stage. It let the audience know the scene was over and they could evaluate what they'd just seen and respond accordingly.

Now, as far as sound goes, the best policy is to teach your actors how to project their voices without any artificial help (translated from the Greek, "artificial help" means a "sound system"). However, if your auditorium is very large, there will be no recourse but to amplify your players. (But beware! It seems sound systems have an uncanny ability to pick up what you *don't* want them to . . . like an unintentional burp from behind the set. Ah, yes . . . one of **Jeremiah People's** classier moments . . .) Amplification can be done in many ways: wireless mikes, stage condensers, overhead condensers, wired lapel microphones, or a combination of one or more of these systems. We could go on for days about the pros and cons of all of these but we don't have the space and you don't have the endurance (believe us) to read an exhaustive lecture on sound. Just keep it as simple as you can.

Let's say you don't have any money but still need some means of amplification. Let us tell you what the **Jeremiah People** did in the early days. Long before we were able to acquire wireless microphones, we used the regular Shure Sm 58 on a stand to amplify ourselves. Now you might say, "Wasn't that awfully confining?" Yes, it was in a sense, but we made it work. By simply putting the microphone stand next to you and maneuvering around it, people were able to hear every word. And you know what? If the actor ignored the microphone while saying his lines, the audience soon forgot there was a microphone three inches from his/her mouth. I guess what I'm saying is, don't let the technical aspects be a deterrant for doing drama. The most important thing is the actor. The rest is just icing.

JUST DO IT!

Well, we said we'd give you some quick tips, and quick they were. In fact, you may now have a whole new set of questions based on the suggestions we've just given you . . . but that's OK. A number of the answers you're seeking will be best addressed by taking script in hand and just doing drama. Hopefully you'll be able to glean some useful pointers from the prior pages. Soon you'll be on your way to creating and using drama in some new and exciting ways. *Enjoy!*

PART TWO

Sketches

ABOUT THE SKETCHES

These twenty-five sketches have been performed by the **Jeremiah People** in churches throughout the United States. Many use humor, some use satire, and a few zoom right to the heart, but they all explore how faith impacts our everyday actions. You could perform them at youth group meetings, as a lead-in to the Sunday morning sermon, grouped together in a variety show at a church dinner, at retreats or camps, or many other church functions.

Production suggestions at the beginning of each sketch take the guesswork out of performance, but staging can be as elaborate or as simple as you desire. We usually opt for the simpler approach and have found it's every bit as effective.

Performance rights to the sketches are yours upon purchase of the book. Feel free to make as many copies as you need of any of the sketches included here. Remember — this is your group's privilege, and can't be transferred to any other group if they don't buy this book for themselves.

Because many past and present members of the **Jeremiah People** have made these sketches available to your group, we ask that you mention the **Jeremiah People** verbally or in printed form during any production of these sketches.

Good luck and have fun!

NOTE: The numerals running vertically down the left margin of each page of dialog are for the convenience of the director. With these, he/she may easily direct attention to a specific passage.

O N E

Who's Gonna Pray?

WHO'S GONNA PRAY?

"To pray or not to pray," that is the question confronted in this less than Shakespearean sketch about public prayer.

SCENE: This sketch takes place in a crowded restaurant at noontime.

CHARACTERS: THE WAITRESS is a diligent worker intent on serving her customers. She is to be played straight with a touch of a Southern accent.

TERRI is the appointed leader of the new social committee. She is pleasant, trying very hard to lead and please at the same time. She should be played straight and dressed very smartly.

BETTY is very reserved and a little shy but very much a woman of conviction. She is dressed conservatively, perhaps with gloves and a hat.

VERA is very outgoing. Some would even call her loud. Her mannerisms are very broad.

MARLENE is overweight and constantly thinking of food. She is jovial and should be dressed in something that accentuates her weight.

DELBERT is very shy and wimpy. He wears black horn-rimmed glasses and a bow tie. Underneath, though, is a lion ready to roar.

STAGING: The scene should take place around a table dressed like a restaurant. They should be positioned around the back half of the table so the audience can view all of them.

PROPS: Ideally, the sketch should be done with real food. However, it is not absolutely necessary. General table wear is sufficient. A pen, note pad, and tray with glasses are needed for the waitress. A sound effects record could be used for restaurant sounds.

LIGHTING: Normal with a quick blackout at the end.

1   WAITRESS: And country fried steak. Is that everyone? Good.
2   I'll get your beverages. *(Exits)*
3   TERRI: Well, good to have you all here. There's a lot of
4   planning to do for the church's social calendar. So I guess
5   we should get started. *(Starts to eat.)*
6   BETTY: Uh, I don't want to be pushy, Terri, but shouldn't
7   we pray first?
8   TERRI: *(With lettuce leaf hanging out of her mouth)* Uh —oh —
9   ah, certainly. Why don't you do it, Betty?
10 BETTY: Well, I'm a bit shy about praying in public.
11 TERRI: OK, any volunteers? *(No response.)* OK, I see. Well, uh,
12   perhaps it isn't necessary. After all, we're not under law,
13   we're under grace. So . . .
14 BETTY: It's just I can't eat unless this food is blessed.
15 VERA: You know, she's right. My mother used to tell of a lady
16   who didn't pray in a restaurant and she choked on a
17   radish, collapsed in her chef salad, and drowned in her
18   blue cheese dressing. Sort of like Annanias and Sapphira.
19 TERRI: Oh, Vera, that's ridiculous. God didn't choke the
20   lady.
21 VERA: No, the radish did.
22 TERRI: I know, Vera. I heard the story but you're saying God
23   had something to do with it.
24 VERA: Maybe, maybe not. Better to be safe than sorry.
25 TERRI: I just don't feel it's necessary. God looks at our heart.
26   I'm thankful for this food. He knows that. Betty, aren't
27   you thankful for your food? *(BETTY nods yes.)* Delbert,
28   aren't you thankful? *(Nods yes.)* Marlene, aren't you
29   thankful for your food?
30 MARLENE: Oh, yes, but I would be more thankful if it was
31   lasagna instead of the low-cal plate.
32 VERA: But Terri . . .
33 TERRI: OK, let's vote. All who think we should pray, raise your
34   your hand. *(Four do.)* Opposed? *(Only TERRI)* Well, I guess
35   we'll pray. Shall we bow our heads? *(Hesitantly)* Dear Lord . . .

1   **WAITRESS:** *(Interrupting)* **OK, I have your drinks.** *(They all*
2   *snap their heads up, embarrassed, and pretend they were doing*
3   *other things.)* **Two coffees, one iced tea, one Coke, and a**
4   **chocolate shake.** *(Hands shake to MARLENE. Everyone looks*
5   *at her.)*
6   **MARLENE:** **It's a celebration.**
7   **BETTY:** **Of what?**
8   **MARLENE:** **Something very important to me, so I thought a**
9   **little splurge was in order.**
10   **BETTY:** **May we ask the occasion?**
11   **MARLENE:** **Take it from me, it's very important.** *(Reaches for*
12   *shake.)*
13   **TERRI:** *(Moves shake back.)* **You told us to hold you accountable**
14   **to this diet, Marlene. What is it?**
15   **MARLENE:** **Ok, it's the Guava Festival in Ecuador. Our**
16   **family has always celebrated it.** *(Reaches for the shake but*
17   *they pull it back.)* **C'mon girls, this diet is killing me. I'm**
18   **starting to look anorexic.** *(Comes up with idea.)* **Wait!**
19   **Whoever prays, ask God to take the calories away. If any**
20   **two or three gathered together ask for anything, it shall**
21   **be done. C'mon girls, agree with me.**
22   **TERRI:** **It's for your own good.**
23   **MARLENE:** **My mother said that before she gave me an**
24   **enema.**
25   **BETTY:** **Could we pray? My salad is getting warm.**
26   **VERA:** **OK, I'll pray.** *(Quickly dips her fingers in her water and*
27   *sprinkles the food.)* **Amen.** *(They all look at her.)* **I used to be**
28   **Catholic. It's blessed, trust me.**
29   **BETTY:** **I don't think so.**
30   **TERRI:** **OK, then we'll do what we used to do around our**
31   **table.** *(Raises her thumb. All, except MARLENE, quickly catch*
32   *on and do the same. To MARLENE)* **You lose, you have to**
33   **pray.**
34   **MARLENE:** **That's not fair. I didn't know the game. Why do I**
35   **have to talk to God?**

1   TERRI: 'Cause you lost.
2   MARLENE: But I'm a new Christian and I've never prayed in
3   public. I won't know what to say.
4   BETTY: Just say a prayer you learned as a kid.
5   MARLENE: Well, OK. *(They bow their heads.)* **Now I lay me**
6   **down to sleep. I pray the Lord ...**
7   BETTY: That's not going to work.
8   MARLENE: Well, I didn't want to do it in the first place.
9   TERRI: I say, let's just forget it. *(All start to disagree and argue.)*
10   OK! Hold it! Betty, you want to pray but you're too
11   shy, right? *(She nods.)* Marlene, you want to pray but you
12   don't know any prayers? *(She nods.)* Well, who's left?
13   *(Suddenly it dawns on all of them that DELBERT is there and*
14   *they all turn to him.)* Delbert, how about you? I mean, you're
15   the man on the committee.
16   DELBERT: *(Meekly)* Well, I don't know. I'm sort of shy and
17   quiet and not used to doing this sort of thing.
18   TERRI: Oh, that's perfect. I mean, God likes shy, quiet,
19   inexperienced prayers.
20   VERA: Right! A humble heart!
21   DELBERT: Really?
22   BETTY: Oh, sure, Delbert. Why, I bet your prayer will get
23   right through.
24   DELBERT: You think so?
25   TERRI: No doubt in our minds, right girls?
26   ALL: Right!
27   TERRI: You're the man God has chosen for this time.
28   DELBERT: Wow!
29   VERA: Like Abraham and Moses.
30   DELBERT: *(Inspired)* **OK, shall we pray.** *(They all bow their*
31   *heads at which time DELBERT raises his hand and in an*
32   *incredibly loud voice prays.)* **Lord, we come to you on this**
33   **beautiful day ...** *(Immediately all their heads snap up, they*
34   *look around and there's a blackout.)*
35

T W O

Bored

BORED

What are you putting inside your body? This sketch looks at Tom and Keith, who are taught two very different lessons about good health.

SCENE: This sketch takes place in a family room.

CHARACTERS: TOM is a typical teen-age boy who must have
                   a constant diet of food and excitement.
                   KEITH is also a typical teen-age boy who
                   always has a solution.

STAGING: The scene is very simple and should be
                   staged with a couple of chairs or a couch.
                   Also, there should be an exit for the kitchen.

PROPS: A television remote control. TV should be
                   imagined out toward the audience.

LIGHTING: Normal.

1   **TOM:** I'm bored. Isn't there anything else on?
2   **KEITH:** *(Flipping channels)* **Well . . . Home Shopping Network,**
3   **reruns of the Brady Bunch, and an old Yul Brenner film.**
4   *(Sits up.)* **Look, he has hair!**
5   **TOM:** He has a nose too. Who cares?
6   **KEITH:** No, he shaved his head for the "King and I." I've
7   never seen him with hair.
8   **TOM:** Well, I know this has certainly given meaning to my
9   day. Got any other life changing tidbits?
10   **KEITH:** Back off, barf face, it was an interesting observation.
11   **TOM:** *(Gets up and goes to kitchen.)* **How about food? Got any**
12   **food?**
13   **KEITH:** Yeah, Mom just went shopping.
14   **TOM:** What is this stuff?
15   **KEITH:** What?
16   **TOM:** Strained carrot juice, rice protein pops, and carob-
17   flavored tofu?
18   **KEITH:** Mom's a health nut. As she always says, "eat healthy,
19   be healthy."
20   **TOM:** No, she got it wrong . . . "eat this, puke this!" You gotta
21   watch her, Keith. Before long you'll be having dinner in
22   your flower bed. Better yet, at Christmas, forget the turkey
23   — just eat the tree!
24   **KEITH:** Yeah, I know. Sometimes my dad and I get so hungry
25   for a burger, the dog gets nervous. *(Remembering)* **I got**
26   **an idea . . . want to watch a movie?**
27   **TOM:** Where?
28   **KEITH:** Here.
29   **TOM:** What?
30   **KEITH:** You know, *(Smiles)* **a** *movie!*
31   **TOM:** *(Mimics)* **A** *movie?* **What movie . . . "Sound of Music,"**
32   **"Crocodile Dundee," "Peter Pan" . . . what?**
33   **KEITH:** Not that kind of movie. You know an . . .
34   **TOM:** Adult film? *(KEITH nods.)* **You're kidding! How?**
35   **KEITH:** What do you mean, how? Just put it in the machine.

1   TOM: Right! And how am I supposed to do that? I'm not going
2   to go rent one. Old man Walker at the video store knows
3   my dad.
4   KEITH: Don't have to rent one . . . we got some here.
5   TOM: Here! You mean in this house?
6   KEITH: No, in the back yard with the dog! Of course, in the
7   house.
8   TOM: How? Why? Where?
9   KEITH: You forgot who and when.
10   TOM: Who and when?
11   KEITH: They belong to my parents. They're in their room
12   and I know where.
13   TOM: You're kidding! They belong to your parents? *(KEITH*
14   *nods in agreement. TOM in disbelief)* **Weird.**
15   KEITH: What do you say?
16   TOM: *(Pause, thinking it over)* I don't know. I'm not sure.
17   KEITH: What can it hurt? It's just a film. As Dad says, "It's
18   art."
19   TOM: *(Thinking)* **Yeah, I guess you're right. Sure, what could
20   it hurt? It's just a film. It's art.**
21   KEITH: Great! They're under the bed. Go pick one out and
22   I'll get us some carrot juice. You know, "eat healthy, stay
23   healthy."
24
25
26
27
28
29
30
31
32
33
34
35

THREE

Old Folks

OLD FOLKS

Are old age and uselessness synonymous? This sketch looks at usefulness in a wheelchair.

SCENE:	This sketch takes place on the back lawn of a retirement home.
CHARACTERS:	The NURSE is a very competent, uptight lady, not attractive and in need of a good "self lift." MARTY is, on the outside, a "happy-go-lucky, life of the retirement home" kind of guy. On the inside, he's a man that has valiantly faced his own worst fears. MAZZY is, on the outside, a woman bound up by fear and confusion. On the inside, she's a lady ready to give MARTY a run for his life.
STAGING:	This scene takes place Center Stage. Both people are in wheelchairs, so you'll need plenty of space.
PROPS:	Two wheelchairs. If possible, sound effects of children laughing.
LIGHTING:	Normal.

1 MARTY: Whoa, Trigger, park it here.

2 NURSE: I would prefer, Mr. Lee, if you didn't refer to me as a

3 horse. *(Stopping his wheelchair)*

4 MARTY: OK. Just stop me here, Bowser.

5 NURSE: What am I going to do with you? Can't you be nice?

6 MARTY: Oh, loosen up, Hildegard . . . I'm only joking. I tell

7 you, you're as stiff as a three-day-old pair of socks. What

8 do you do for fun . . . read the obituaries?

9 NURSE: I'll have you know, I have my wild side. I just prefer

10 to hide it a little.

11 MARTY: A little? If you hid it any more you'd need a map to

12 find it.

13 NURSE: Well, I'll work on it. It's just I've always been taught

14 a godly woman is supposed to be submissive, humble,

15 and quiet.

16 MARTY: Submissive, maybe, but not comatose. Put a smile

17 on your face. *(She does.)* That's better! See? You're a pretty

18 girl when you smile.

19 NURSE: You really think so?

20 MARTY: Oh, absolutely. *(She smiles and exits. As she does he*

21 *pulls his hands out from under the blanket on his lap and*

22 *uncrosses his fingers. Looks up to the sky as if speaking to God.)*

23 It was for a good cause. *(MAZZY pulls up in a wheelchair*

24 *next to him.)* Howdy. I haven't seen you around. New here?

25 *(MAZZY gives no response. MARTY looks at her wheelchair.)*

26 Nice wheels.

27 MAZZY: I beg your pardon?

28 MARTY: What! Did I belch? *(Laughs)* I said nice wheels.

29 Your wheelchair is a nice model. I've seen it in Geriatric

30 Trends Magazine. It won Domestic Chair of the Year.

31 *(MAZZY gives no response.)* Talker, aren't you?

32 MAZZY: I beg your pardon?

33 MARTY: Thanks, just a little gas. *(Looking for response)* Nice

34 day, huh?

35 MAZZY: I beg your pardon?

1	MARTY:	What! Did I . . . oh, wait, I've already used that one.
2		You win. If you stick around, I'm gonna have to come up
3		with some new ones. I've never had more than one "I beg
4		your pardon" in a conversation. I'm Marty Lee of the
5		General Lee clan. And you're . . ? *(MAZZY just sits ignoring*
6		*him.)* Don't tell me . . . of the Helen Keller clan. *(Starts to*
7		*imitate sign language and speaks real loud.)* Nice to meet you.
8	MAZZY:	*(Trying to hold back a smile)* Nice to meet you.
9	MARTY:	*(Speaking at the top of his voice)* She talks! She knows
10		the English language!
11	MAZZY:	Be quiet, Mr. Lee! I do not wish to have attention
12		drawn to me.
13	MARTY:	Good. I hate to share the spotlight. *(They both laugh.)*
14		So what is your name?
15	MAZZY:	My name is Mazzy Armor.
16	MARTY:	As in the hot dog?
17	MAZZY:	I beg your pardon?
18	MARTY:	Oh no, we're back to that.
19	MAZZY:	No, we're not back to that. I just didn't quite catch
20		what you said.
21	MARTY:	Oh, I said as in hot dog. You know Armour Hot Dogs?
22	MAZZY:	No. What are they? One of those rock and roll bands?
23	MARTY:	They're weenies. You know weenies, don't you?
24	MAZZY:	I'm not personally acquainted but, since they're
25		your friends, if you bring them by, I'll be cordial.
26	MARTY:	*(Looks at her confused)* So what's a good-looking girl
27		like you doing in a place like this?
28	MAZZY:	Sitting, and I can't believe you used that line. It's as
29		old as the hills.
30	MARTY:	You're kidding — I thought I made it up!
31	MAZZY:	Perhaps you did. I said it was as old as the hills.
32	MARTY:	Oh, you got me. You're pretty sharp. I think we'll
33		get along just fine.
34	MAZZY:	Well, maybe, but I won't be around long.
35	MARTY:	Around here not many will.

1   MAZZY: I didn't mean death. I meant I'll be leaving for home
2   as soon as I heal a little. You see, I broke my hip some
3   time ago and my children thought it would be better if I
4   recuperated here. But as soon as I can get out of this
5   blasted chair, I'm going back to being useful.
6   MARTY: I see. Well, when you leave can I have your chair?
7   I could win the ten-meter roll on Founder's Day with that
8   piece of machinery.
9   MAZZY: When I leave, Mr. Lee, you may have my chair, my
10   room, anything you want. I won't be needing it . . . and I
11   won't be looking back.
12   MARTY: Afraid you'll turn into a pillar of salt, huh?
13   MAZZY and MARTY: *(In unison)* I beg your pardon?
14   MARTY: You know you've really got to find a new line. How
15   about, "Say it again, sucka?" *(Pause)* So, you're
16   recuperating? When did you break your hip?
17   MAZZY: As I said, it was some time ago but God is healing it
18   every day. He wants us useful not useless. As long as I'm
19   in this chair, I'm useless . . . so obviously it's not his will.
20   MARTY: Obviously. *(Pause)* Have you ever considered the
21   possibility that it might not heal?
22   MAZZY: To consider that possibility is to throw away faith.
23   So the answer is no. How about you? Are you faithless
24   or faithful?
25   MARTY: I'm Baptist.
26   MAZZY: Mr. Lee, you are avoiding my question.
27   MARTY: I am? Could you repeat it, please?
28   MAZZY: There is no need. I know full well you're playing cat
29   and mouse with me. I was a school teacher for forty years
30   and I can tell when the mouse is hiding the cheese.
31   MARTY: Hide the cheese? *(She glares at him.)* OK. I'll answer
32   the question. God's will isn't . . . how can I say this? God
33   doesn't want death or growing old or cancer or wars or
34   hungry people or anchovies. *(She looks at him.)* I thought
35   I'd throw that in. I've never know anyone who liked them,

1   so I figure God doesn't either, but those things still
2   happen. Someday those things won't be around, but until
3   he comes back, they will.

4   MAZZY: What you're saying is God won't heal me!

5   MARTY: No, I'm not saying that. God and I have a deal . . . I
6   don't decide things for him and he takes all the calories
7   away when I have a Snickers at three in the morning.
8   What I'm saying is, Mazzy, if you don't get up and walk
9   tomorrow, will you still be useful?

10   MAZZY: Impossible! You can't be useful in a wheelchair! If
11   this is the way it's going to be then . . .

12   MARTY: Then what? You'll renounce your faith or just curse
13   God and call it quits. *(She looks at him rather sternly.)* **Look,**
14   I understand what you're goin' through. I didn't plan to
15   be in a wheelchair either. I was a farmer. It was very
16   difficult to go from running a one hundred twenty acre
17   farm to a bedpan, but that's what happened.

18   MAZZY: It's not fair! It's just not fair!

19   MARTY: No, it's not, but who said it would be? I think we get
20   how it's gonna be in the kingdom mixed up with what
21   we think it should be here. If here was perfect, then
22   there'd be no need for heaven. Mazzy, you can be useful.
23   *(She looks at him with doubt.)* **You can! Every Wednesday,**
24   that's today . . .

25   MAZZY: I know what day it is, Mr. Lee.

26   MARTY: Every Wednesday a group of kids come here and we
27   help them with their lessons. They don't have any
28   parents. They're from the orphanage across the street.
29   We play their grandparents and help them out a bit. You
30   bein' a school teacher, I bet you could really make a
31   difference.

32   MAZZY: I can't run anywhere. I'm stuck in this infernal chair.
33   How can I teach when I can't get around?

34   MARTY: You're not teaching them basketball — you're
35   teaching them to read.

1 MAZZY: I don't know, Mr. Lee — this is not ideal.
2 MARTY: Mazzy, *ideal* won't come until Gabriel blows the
3 trumpet. *(Sound of kids)* Well, you'd better decide soon
4 'cause they're here. I gotta run. *(Starts to roll then turns*
5 *back and looks at her.)* Well?
6 MAZZY: *(Looks at him; thinks.)* Race you!
7 MARTY: You're gonna lose old woman. This chariot ain't
8 pretty but it's got a lot of horsepower.
9 MAZZY: *(Rolling ahead of him)* Say it again, sucka!
10
11
12
13
14
15
16
17
18
19
20
21
22
23
24
25
26
27
28
29
30
31
32
33
34
35

F O U R

The Twenty-Year Reunion

THE TWENTY-YEAR REUNION

A sketch in which Bonnie and Jason look at years gone by and ask "what if?"

SCENE:	This sketch takes place both outside and inside a hotel ballroom where a high school reunion is taking place.
CHARACTERS:	BARRY is a typical 38-year-old man who would do anything for his wife. BONNIE is Barry's wife. It's her reunion and she's both apprehensive and excited about the evening. FINNEY is a short, stocky loudmouth. He is very physical and is always looking for someone to punch on. MAX is Finney's old friend. He should be, in appearance, the opposite of Barry. SYLVIA is Finney's wife and certainly his equal. She's the only one who can keep him in line. She is loud, brash, and very friendly. JASON is Bonnie's old flame. He is very good looking and very well dressed. Even though he has a smile on the outside, something is missing on the inside.
STAGING:	At first, the scene takes place outside the doors of the ballroom. This can be done by putting a door frame on-stage, or by pantomiming the opening of the door to signify two separate rooms. Ideally, the main stage is set with table, punch bowl and glasses. However, the props can be pantomimed.
PROPS:	All are optional: Door frame; table, punch bowl and glasses; sound effects of a party.
LIGHTING:	Two distinct spots, if possible — Stage Left and Center. When Bonnie and Barry enter the party, the Stage Left spot would go to black. Otherwise the lighting is normal.

1 BARRY: Honey, you'll be the best-looking one there.

2 BONNIE: You have to say that — you're my husband.

3 BARRY: Trust me. Why would I lie?

4 BONNIE: Because you hate sleeping on the couch.

5 BARRY: Well, that's true, but I'm not lying this time.

6 BONNIE: This time! Have there been other times? When?

7 You really do hate my dress, don't you?

8 BARRY: No! It's great! Relax . . . it's your twenty-year high

9 school reunion and you'll be the most beautiful one there.

10 Guaranteed. *(Reassuringly gives her a kiss.)*

11 BONNIE: You really think so?

12 BARRY: I know so. Now suck it up and let's go in.

13 BONNIE: *(Paranoid)* Suck what up? My stomach! It's pooching

14 out! Oh no, I'm a cow! I knew I should . . .

15 BARRY: I'm sorry, hon. Suck up has nothing to do with you.

16 It's an old football expression. Your stomach is fine.

17 BONNIE: No, it's not. It's in one big knot and it's poochie.

18 Stay with me, Barry.

19 BARRY: OK. Here we go. Ready? Five - four - three - two - one

20 — blast off! *(They go through the door into the party. No one*

21 *notices.)* See, it's just a quiet party made up of nice, quiet,

22 middle-aged . . .

23 FINNEY: *(Charging up to BARRY)* Max! Max, you dog! How are

24 you?! *(Slaps him on the back.)* Long time no see. Put up

25 your dukes! *(Jokingly begins to punch at BARRY.)* Watch me

26 fade! Watch me fade! Too fast for you, huh?

27 BARRY: Excuse me, but . . . excuse me! *(Bobbing and weaving*

28 *trying to get out of FINNEY's way)* I'm not Max!

29 FINNEY: Yeah and I'm Mother Teresa. Put 'em up! *(Laughs)*

30 BARRY: No really! I'm Bar . . . *(FINNEY lands a punch in*

31 *BARRY's stomach)* . . . ry! *(Gasping for air)*

32 FINNEY: *(Laughing)* Hey, hey, Maxy boy, you forgot to cover!

33 BARRY: *(Still gasping)* I'm not Maxy! I'm . . .

34 MAX: Finney! *(Comes up to FINNEY.)* Finney, my old buddy!

35 FINNEY: Maxy! Hey, hey!

1   **MAX:**   Put 'em up! *(They laugh and exit punching at each other.)*

2   **BONNIE:**   Hon! Hon! Are you all right? I'm so sorry!

3   **BARRY:**   Who was that . . . Attila the Hun?

4   **BONNIE:**   No, it was Finney Wheeler . . . class animal. I'm

5   sorry. How's your stomach?

6   **BARRY:**   I don't know. Would you look behind me — he shoved

7   it back just above my rear.

8   **BONNIE:**   I'm sorry.

9   **BARRY:**   Excuse me, sweetheart, I'm going to the bathroom.

10   You're on your own. I've got to check on my belly button.

11   I think he knocked it into my socks. *(Exits)*

12   **BONNIE:**   Yeah . . . OK. Don't be gone long. *(Moves to punch*

13   *table.)*

14   **JASON:**   *(From behind)* **Bonnie?! Bonnie Burton?!**

15   **BONNIE:**   *(Turns and becomes nervous.)* **Jason.**

16   **JASON:**   Aren't you beautiful!

17   **BONNIE:**   *(Smiles)* **Thank you. And you're . . . it's Martin.**

18   **JASON:**   Martin?

19   **BONNIE:**   My last name. I'm Bonnie Martin but you can call

20   me . . .

21   **JASON:**   Beautiful. How have you been?

22   **BONNIE:**   You always were the charmer . . . and I'm nervous.

23   *(Smiles)*

24   **JASON:**   About what?

25   **BONNIE:**   About looking twenty years older.

26   **JASON:**   *(Laugh)* **No need to worry. You look great!**

27   **SYLVIA:**   *(Moving to table, shouting behind her)* **Do you want the**

28   **ones with crust or the ones without?** *(Bumping into*

29   *BONNIE)* **Oh, I'm sorry. I need to get . . .** *(Noticing BONNIE)*

30   **Bonnie?! Bonnie Burton?!** *(Yelling back)* **Finney, it's**

31   **Bonnie Burton!** *(To BONNIE)* **I can't believe it. You look**

32   **like yesterday.** *(Yelling back)* **Finney, she looks like**

33   **yesterday, doesn't she?** *(To BONNIE)* **He's an animal.**

34   *(Yelling back)* **Stop punching that statue! It cost a fortune!**

35   *(To BONNIE)* **Punching, always punching. Bonnie, you**

1   look like yesterday. Oh, I already said that . . . well
2   whatever. How are you? How are you? Where are you?
3   You're so skinny. I was born with more meat on my bones.
4   You haven't been sick, have you?
5 BONNIE: No.
6 SYLVIA: Anorexic?
7 BONNIE: No.
8 SYLVIA: You're poor, can't afford food. Oh, I'm so sorry.
9   *(Yelling back)* Finney! Stop slapping old Mrs. Wardlow and
10   bring me a couple of dollars.
11 BONNIE: Sylvia, I'm fine . . . really. I just look like this.
12 SYLVIA: No one just looks like this. Well, whatever. *(Hugs*
13   *her.)* Great to see you! I have thought about you so much.
14   You married?
15 BONNIE: Yeah, his name is . . .
16 SYLVIA: *(Noticing JASON, then interrupting)* Jason Turner! I
17   can't believe it! Don't tell me . . . you two actually got
18   married! They said it would never last but I didn't believe
19   them. My gosh, you're both gorgeous! What do your kids
20   look like, Ken and Barbie?
21 BONNIE: Syl . . . Jason and I aren't married.
22 SYLVIA: Divorced? I'm so . . .
23 BONNIE: No, we're not.
24 SYLVIA: *(Skeptical)* Just living together?
25 BONNIE: *(Laughs)* No.
26 SYLVIA: Well, how did you get the kids?
27 BONNIE: We don't have kids . . . actually I have kids but *we*
28   don't have kids.
29 SYLVIA: Isn't that the way it is. You haul them around for
30   nine months and you raise them too. *(Slaps JASON on the*
31   *arm.)* I can't believe it! All you men are the same. Finney
32   never helps. When I was ready to deliver, he was watching
33   championship wrestling. I had to get him in a spinning toe
34   hold to get his attention. No joke! He's never around. The
35   kids think he's an old prize fighter that shows up for dinner.

1 BONNIE: Syl, Jason and I never got married. I married
2   someone else . . . his name is Barry Martin.
3 SYLVIA: *(Looking at JASON)* Is this true? *(JASON nods.)* Are
4   you single? Happy? Available? You like kids? I've got four
5   but maybe we can sell them off. *(They all laugh.)* No, huh?
6   Well, whatever. I love Finney . . . he's big, he's loud, but
7   he's . . . *(Thinks)* big, he's loud . . . *(Laughs)*
8 FINNEY: *(Off-stage)* Sylvia!
9 SYLVIA: *(Turning, yelling)* Keep your shirt on! *(To BONNIE)*
10   Well, I'd better get these sandwiches and take them to
11   Sasquatch. You know — give him something to do with
12   his hands. Good seeing you both. Gosh, you're gorgeous!
13   *(Turns and yells.)* Stop punching that, Finney, you want
14   to get arrested? *(SYLVIA exits.)*
15 BONNIE: *(Both laughing)* Are you married?
16 JASON: No.
17 BONNIE: Happy?
18 JASON: *(Long look)* Compared to what? *(Laughs)*
19 BONNIE: Funny isn't it . . . coming back after twenty years?
20 JASON: Yeah, it's a rush with the past.
21 BONNIE: Huh?
22 JASON: It seems like yesterday, yet it seems a million years
23   ago. Time doesn't stand still.
24 BONNIE: Neither do the wrinkles. They keep marching on.
25   *(Both laugh.)* Jason, have you ever . . . ?
26 JASON: Bonnie . . . it's strange . . .
27 BONNIE: *(Laughs)* You first.
28 JASON: No, beauty before . . . whatever. *(Laughs)*
29 BONNIE: I was going to ask whether you've ever married.
30 JASON: No, thought about it once, but . . .
31 BONNIE: Cold feet?
32 JASON: Or cold heart.
33 BONNIE: Cold heart?
34 JASON: Yeah, she was the most beautiful girl I've ever known.
35   I just didn't know if I was ready.

1   BONNIE: That's not being cold, that's being wise.

2   JASON: Sometimes I wonder. *(Pause)* So, you're married?

3   BONNIE: Yes, and I have two children. Marian's eleven and

4   Jason's nine.

5   JASON: Jason, huh? Good name. *(Pause)*

6   BONNIE: Jason, I find it awkward ...

7   JASON: Bonnie, I've really ...

8   BONNIE: Your turn.

9   JASON: No, you. I'm a chauvinist.

10   BONNIE: I find it awkward standing here talking to you.

11   JASON: Why?

12   BONNIE: Memories ... feelings.

13   JASON: I know. It was twenty years ago but it feels like

14   yesterday.

15   BONNIE: Jason, I don't think it's good to talk about this.

16   JASON: I need to. For twenty years I've waited to see you ...

17   to explain to you ...

18   BONNIE: *(Interrupting)* Jason.

19   JASON: Bonnie ... back then ... uh ... I was a kid, you

20   know. I felt ... well ... I felt I had the world on a string.

21   Commitment ... to one person ... well ... I just couldn't ...

22   BONNIE: That's in the past.

23   JASON: But it still influences me today. Bon, haven't you

24   ever sat and wondered "what if"?

25   BONNIE: *(Obviously uneasy about talking)* Jason ...

26   JASON: You know, what if you and I ... *(BARRY enters, a little*

27   *paranoid.)*

28   BARRY: *(Looking around)* You don't see him anywhere, do you?

29   BONNIE: Jason, this is my husband Barry. Barry, this is Jason.

30   BARRY: *(Shakes hand.)* Nice to meet you, Jason.

31   JASON: You too, Barry.

32   BONNIE: Want some punch, hon?

33   BARRY: I've already had one, thanks. *(Rubs stomach.)*

34   BONNIE: We were just talking about the past. *(Looking at*

35   *JASON)* About the choices we made and how there's no

1   going back.
2   BARRY: Reunions can be a real trip, huh? All the memories.
3   I went to mine last year. I couldn't get over how much
4   everyone had changed.
5   JASON: Nothing stays the same ... *(Pause)* and you can't go
6   back, can you? *(They all look at each other.)*
7   SYLVIA: *(Off-stage)* OK, everyone ... *(Sing)* "Should old
8   acquaintance be forgot and ..." *(Continue and fade.)*
9
10
11
12
13
14
15
16
17
18
19
20
21
22
23
24
25
26
27
28
29
30
31
32
33
34
35

FIVE

$ 685.00 Air Filter

$685.00 AIR FILTER

A sketch in which "brotherly love" is thrown out the window for a dollar . . . or should we say dollars.

SCENE: This sketch takes place in a repair garage.

CHARACTERS: BUCK is a down-home car repairman whose ethics are more than questionable.
                 VICKI is the naive but very trusting wife of Buck's Bible study partner.

STAGING: The scene should take place Center Stage.

PROPS: A clipboard and pencil.

LIGHTING: Normal.

1   BUCK: Yes, Ma'am, may I . . . *(Looking up, recognizes her.)* **Why,**
2   **Vicki! How are you this morning?**
3   VICKI: **Good morning, Buck. Just fine. How's Florence?**
4   BUCK: **Oh, fine, fine. What can we do for you this morning?**
5   VICKI: **Well, Bob wanted me to bring the car in and have you**
6   **change an . . . air filter?**
7   BUCK: **Oh, that should be no problem. We're kind of busy**
8   **this morning, but I figure anything for old . . . Bob-a-**
9   **roons!** *(Chuckles)* **Let's see, let me lift up the hood and see**
10   **what we've got here.** *(Mimes opening hood and unscrewing*
11   *air filter — continues to work as he talks.)* **Ah, there we go.**
12   **Hey, did Bob tell you about the great Bible study we had**
13   **the other night?**
14   VICKI: **Oh, yes . . . he really enjoyed that.**
15   BUCK: **Yeah, so did I. Really blessed my heart.** *(Pause — then*
16   *he returns to work.)*
17   VICKI: **He said this wouldn't be too expensive.**
18   BUCK: **No, I figure about fifteen dollars or so.**
19   VICKI: **Oh, good. About how long will this take?**
20   BUCK: **Oh, I imagine just a couple of minutes; couldn't be**
21   **simpler. This is a mighty fine car you've got here.**
22   VICKI: **Well, thank you. Bob's out of town for a few days and**
23   **he just wanted me to have it fixed by the time he got back.**
24   BUCK: *(Slow and thoughtful)* **Oh, Bob's out of town?**
25   VICKI: **Yes.**
26   BUCK: **I see.** *(Pause . . . slowly)* **Well, Vicki, I don't know how to**
27   **tell you this, and I hate to be the bringer of bad news but**
28   **we've got a lot bigger problem on our hands than just an**
29   **air filter.**
30   VICKI: **Oh?**
31   BUCK: **Well, I didn't see it when I first lifted up the hood, but**
32   **well . . .** *(Pointing)* **you can see there that the carburetor's**
33   **all clogged up and the plugs . . . are shot, and the fan belt's**
34   **broken, and . . . the cable to the battery's corroded. It's a**
35   **mess. Say, you ever notice when you kinda come to a stop**

1   **you get that chu-ga-chu-ga sound?**
2   **VICKI: Well . . . no . . .**
3   **BUCK: That's a sure sign. We'll probably have to pull the**
4   **whole engine out of it. And the muffler! I don't know how**
5   **you got this thing in here. It's just terrible.**
6   **VICKI: Well . . . how much work is this going to involve?**
7   **BUCK: All depends on what we find when we tear the**
8   **transmission out of it.**
9   **VICKI: *(Shocked)* Tra . . . transmission!**
10   **BUCK: It's shot to pieces.** *(Pulls a piece of paper from his pocket.)*
11   **Listen, why don't you just sign right here on this estimate**
12   **and we can begin work.**
13   **VICKI: Well . . . uh . . . can't we wait till my husband gets**
14   **back?**
15   **BUCK: *(Acts concerned)* Now, Vicki, let me be honest with you.**
16   **I . . . really don't know how I'd be able to face Bob if I let**
17   **you drive out of here in this . . . this death trap.**
18   **VICKI: *(Frightened)* You mean . . . ?**
19   **BUCK: *(Placating)* No . . . no . . . now go ahead. If you want to**
20   **leave, don't let me be the one to stop you . . . but I'm sure**
21   **that your medical insurance is paid up . . .**
22   **VICKI: *(Frantically)* Where do I sign?** *(Blackout)*
23
24
25
26
27
28
29
30
31
32
33
34
35

SIX

Call Me Any Time

CALL ME ANY TIME

A scene that asks, "When does our service to God interfere with our service for God?"

CHARACTERS: SAM is an overly busy Christian with mixed-up priorities.
MICK is a person who needs someone to talk to and who cares.

STAGING: The scene is very basic. Sam and Mick should be on opposite ends of the stage.

PROPS: Two phones. (optional)

LIGHTING: Normal.

1   **SAM:**   *(Picks up phone.)* **Hello.**

2   **MICK:**   **Hello, Sam? This is Mick. I . . .**

3   **SAM:**   **Hey, Mick, great to hear from you, man! Listen, I hate**

4   **to cut you off, but I was just heading out the door on my**

5   **way to a finance committee meeting at the church.**

6   **MICK:**   *(Disappointed)* **Oh, well . . . I . . . just kind of needed**

7   **somebody to talk to . . . uh . . .**

8   **SAM:**   *(Thoughtfully)* **Well . . . how about tomorrow?**

9   **MICK:**   **Tonight would be a lot better.**

10   **SAM:**   **No, wait, wait. Tomorrow I've got Outreach class. Hey,**

11   **listen, we've had some fantastic discussions on**

12   **community involvement and personal counseling! You**

13   **ought to make it out sometime. It's been great!**

14   **MICK:**   *(Discouraged)* **Yeah, sure, Sam, I'll . . .**

15   **SAM:**   **Now, Friday, we . . . no, no, Friday I promised to help**

16   **fix the new volleyball pits at church. But Saturday**

17   **would . . . no, Saturday morning I've got men's prayer**

18   **breakfast. But Saturday afternoon . . . hey, listen,**

19   **Saturday afternoon, Mick . . . but make sure it's before**

20   **6:00 because, well . . . I'm sure you understand. I wouldn't**

21   **want to miss volleyball practice. We've got a new singles**

22   **league started. Slammin' Sammy, they call me. I'll count**

23   **on talking to you on Saturday, OK? Take care, man. I'll**

24   **be prayin' for you.** *(Hangs up phone and freezes in position.)*

25   **MICK:**   *(Slow, as if holding back tears)* **Yeah, thanks, Sam.**

26   *(Blackout)*

27

28

29

30

31

32

33

34

35

SEVEN

The Elevator

THE ELEVATOR

A scene in which Jim and Chuck are stuck in an elevator and examine what it means to trust in the Lord.

SCENE: This sketch takes place in an elevator.

CHARACTERS: JIM is a seemingly confident Christian until his faith is put to the test.
CHUCK is a Christian who knows God is in control, and is certain Jim has lost control.

STAGING: The scene is done Center Stage in a confined area to simulate an elevator.

PROPS: A hat for Chuck. (optional)

LIGHTING: Normal.

1   **CHUCK:** **All the way to the bottom floor?**

2   **JIM:** **Right.**

3   **CHUCK:** *(Pauses, does a double take. A smile comes across his face*

4   *as he recognizes JIM.)* **Say, aren't you ... ?**

5   **JIM:** *(Grabs CHUCK's hand and shakes it rapidly, not letting go.)*

6   **That's right, I'm Jim Carson. I haven't seen you since you**

7   **moved. How ya been?**

8   **CHUCK:** *(Still shaking hands as arm starts to go limp)* **Just fine.**

9   **You work all the way up here on the forty-eighth floor?**

10   **JIM:** **Oh no, no ... I've been out sharing.**

11   **CHUCK:** **Really? Out sharing what?** *(CHUCK grabs JIM's hand*

12   *to stop the arm pumping and is obviousl, a little pooped.)*

13   **JIM:** **I thought you'd never ask.** *(Smirkingly laughs.)* **I've been**

14   **out telling people about the great speaker we have at our**

15   **church this week. His name is Hal Fipple and he's really**

16   **fantastic.** *(Pauses and thinks.)* **Say, you know you ought to**

17   **come tonight. I think you'd really ...**

18   **CHUCK:** *(Laughs nervously)* **Well ... uh ... I ... uh ... we've**

19   **got company coming ... a Bible study. That's right, a**

20   **Bible study and I don't think we can make it.**

21   **JIM:** **That's fine. How about tomorrow night?**

22   **CHUCK:** **Well ... uh ... to be honest with you, this approach**

23   **to Christianity and all is just not what I'm into.**

24   **JIM:** **Oh, but Chuck, Hal Fipple has something for everyone.**

25   **Why, he's been teaching us some great things about faith.**

26   **You know, learning how to trust in the Lord. How to rely**

27   **on him at all times. You know, just how to relax in all**

28   **situations. It will change your life, because Chuck, it**

29   **works. It really works.** *(Suddenly they both jerk and almost*

30   *fall down. They straighten up and look around.)* **What**

31   **happened?**

32   **CHUCK:** **I think the elevator broke down.**

33   **JIM:** *(Instant panic)* **Broke down?!**

34   **CHUCK:** *(Relaxed)* **Yes, but it happens all the time.**

35   **JIM:** *(Still panicky)* **Well, it's never happened to me before!**

1   **CHUCK:**   **There's no need to get excited. In about fifteen or**
2   **twenty minutes someone will come to ...**
3   **JIM:**   *(Even more panicky)* **Fifteen or twenty minutes?! Chuck,**
4   **we've got to get out of here.** *(Fumbling for an excuse)* **Hal**
5   **Fipple needs me! There's got to be a way to get this thing**
6   **running.** *(He moves in front of CHUCK, pushing him out of the*
7   *way. He pantomimes pushing the various floor buttons slowly,*
8   *then faster until finally he's pounding on the entire board.)*
9   **CHUCK:**   **Would you stop that? You keep that up and we'll**
10   **never get out of here.**
11   **JIM:**   **There's got to be a way we can talk to somebody.**
12   **CHUCK:**   *(Slightly perturbed)* **There is. There's a little phone**
13   **behind there.** *(Points to an imaginary door on the panel.)* **That**
14   **connects you to the bottom floor.**
15   **JIM:**   *(Mimes grabbing the phone.)* **Hello ... hello ...** *(Calm*
16   *and relieved)* **Yes ...** *(Panicked and yelling)* **We're trapped!**
17   **Get us out of here!**
18   **CHUCK:**   *(Grabs the phone out of his hand. Looks disgustedly at*
19   *JIM.)* **Yes, we're in elevator number three, stuck between**
20   **the twenty-seventh and twenty-eighth floors ... that's**
21   **right ... right ... there's two of us ... right, as soon as**
22   **you could, we would appreciate it ... right ... thanks**
23   **very much.** *(Hangs up the phone.)*
24   **JIM:**   **Well, what did he say?**
25   **CHUCK:**   **He said he would get somebody on it as soon as he**
26   **could.**
27   **JIM:**   *(Grabs the phone back off the panel.)* **Hello ... hello ... yes**
28   **... listen, Hal Fipple needs me!** *(Pause)* **Fipple ... Fip-pull**
29   **... that's "F" as in fix, "I" as in immediately, two "P's," as**
30   **in pretty please, "L" as in lousy, "E" as in elevator ...**
31   *Idiot!* *(Hangs up phone. Mimes feeling walls and follows wall*
32   *behind CHUCK. CHUCK turns to tell him something and by*
33   *this time, JIM is on his opposite side.)*
34   **CHUCK:**   *(Moving to the side where JIM was)* **Listen, would you**
35   **just ...** *(Looks up and realizes JIM isn't there. Slightly surprised,*

1   *he looks around, finally to his left, sees JIM and in a slapstick*
2   *way hits him.)* **Would you just settle down?** *(Deliberately)*
3   **There's no need to get excited, just stand there, relax,**
4   **and be . . . calm!** *(JIM pauses, then moves toward CHUCK as*
5   *if to say "But.")* **Calm!**
6   **JIM:**   **Calm.** *(CHUCK nods with a smile. JIM then ponders the*
7   *thought, during which time his face and body begin to show*
8   *increasing panic and shaking until finally he screams.)* **Ahhh!**
9   *(The unexpected scream obviously scares CHUCK.)* **Listen,**
10   **Chuck, maybe if we jump . . . come on, let's jump!** *(He grabs*
11   *CHUCK's armpit and begins to jump, lifting them both off the*
12   *ground.)*
13   **CHUCK:**   *(With a shocked look on his face and finally at his wit's*
14   *end)* **Would you knock . . . it . . . off! What are you . . . crazy?**
15   **Now look, there's no way we're going to get out of here for**
16   **awhile, absolutely no way. The only way I've ever seen**
17   **anybody try and get out of a situation like this was in some**
18   **dumb movie where this guy tries to climb out of this trap**
19   **door** *(Pointing to the ceiling)* **and even then he didn't . . .** *(JIM*
20   *leaps on CHUCK's back and tries to reach the ceiling. In the process,*
21   *he is choking CHUCK with one arm. Shocked and choking . . .)*
22   **Would you get off?!** *(JIM falls to the floor. He picks himself up*
23   *and brushes himself off.)*
24   **JIM:**   **Really, Chuck. There's no need to be violent.**
25   **CHUCK:**   **Violent!** *(Surprised and crazed)* **Violent?! What was all**
26   **this stuff you were telling me just a few minutes ago**
27   **about trusting in the Lord — relying on him always and**
28   **relaxing in all situations!** *(Both JIM and CHUCK jerk again*
29   *as if the elevator has started and they look around the*
30   *compartment, finally looking at the floor numbers lighting up.)*
31   **JIM:**   *(Happily)* **We're moving!**
32   **CHUCK:**   **Well, finally.**
33   **JIM:**   *(Pauses thoughtfully.)* **Praise the Lord! See, Chuck, what**
34   **trusting the Lord can do?** *(CHUCK looks at the audience in*
35   *despair. Blackout.)*

EIGHT

The Party

THE PARTY

A scene in which Kathy goes to a party to find someone to talk to and ends up getting less than she bargained for.

SCENE: This sketch takes place at a big noisy party.

CHARACTERS: DENNIS thinks he's a lady killer, but is really obnoxious.
KATHY is a reserved but friendly girl looking for someone to care.
JOHN is a Christian friend of Dennis' on his way home.

STAGING: The scene takes place Center Stage.

PROPS: Two folding chairs; optional party material.

LIGHTING: Normal.

1   DENNIS: **Excuse me!** *(He smiles as KATHY turns and looks at*
2   *him somewhat sheepishly.)* **Hi! Is that seat taken?** *(Points to*
3   *empty seat beside her.)*
4   KATHY: **Uh — no.**
5   DENNIS: *(Slides like a snake into it.)* **It is now!** *(He sits there with a*
6   *big grin, checking her out.)* **I'm Dennis.**
7   KATHY: *(Hesitantly)* **I'm Kathy.**
8   DENNIS: *(With a coy smile)* **You certainly are! Well, say, you're**
9   **kind of new to this area, aren't you?**
10   KATHY: **We just moved here.**
11   DENNIS: **We?**
12   KATHY: **Yeah, my folks and I . . . I'm single.**
13   DENNIS: **Oh, really? Well, uh, who'd you come to the party**
14   **with?**
15   KATHY: **I came with Pam,** *(Looks around)* **but I don't see her**
16   **anywhere.**
17   DENNIS: **Oh, don't worry about Pam . . . she's a real swinger.**
18   **Yeah, good old Pam. We call her "hinges," 'cause she's**
19   **something to "a-door!"** *(Laughing)* **Get it? Hinges . . . a-**
20   **door . . .** *(Laughing dies off quickly with no response.)* **Well,**
21   **say, uh, what do you do besides just sit there and look good?**
22   KATHY: **I work at the telephone company.**
23   DENNIS: **Oh, really? Well, that doesn't surprise me 'cause I**
24   **know you really "push my buttons."** *(Laughs at his*
25   *cleverness.)*
26   KATHY: **What do you do?**
27   DENNIS: *(Laughs quickly — stops.)* **Uh, uh . . . I'm into . . . uh,**
28   **publications.**
29   KATHY: **What area?**
30   DENNIS: **Huh? Oh, I, uh . . . I work in a** *(Under his breath)*
31   **Christian** *(Back to normal volume)* **bookstore.** *(Quickly)* **Say,**
32   **you know, you strike me as a girl with a lot of diversified**
33   **interests. I mean, I'm a guy with a lot of diversified**
34   **interests! That's right . . . I like to do all kinds of**
35   **things . . . especially sports. I mean, I like to hike, camp**

1   **and ski. I play football, soccer, hockey . . . wrestling. Yes**

2   **siree, I love it all, as long as it involves a little, uh, physical**

3   **activity.** *(Smiles — anxiously awaits a response.)*

4   **KATHY:** **Well, I like literature.**

5   **DENNIS:** *(Smile disappears.)* **Uh, oh yeah, me too! Nothing**

6   **better than a good book I always say! Out there hiking,**

7   **camping, skiing, out on the old basketball court . . . I've**

8   **always got a book.** *(Chuckles)*

9   **KATHY:** **My favorite is poetry.**

10   **DENNIS:** *(Smile again freezes, then disappears with kind of a sick*

11   *look.)* **Poetry? Poetry . . . oh, yeah, one of my favorites,**

12   **poetry . . . uh . . .** *(Trying to remember a poem)* **. . . OK.**

13   **Little fly upon the wall**

14   **Ain't you got no clothes at all?**

15   **Ain't you got no woolen shirt?**

16   **Ain't you got no pretty skirt?**

17   **Little fly, aren't you cold?**

18   *(Laughs cleverly.)* **That's a little free verse.** *(Laughs)*

19   **Speaking of free, what are you doing after the party, huh?**

20   **KATHY:** *(Nervously)* **Oh, well, I really have to go . . .** *(She starts*

21   *to move as if to leave.)*

22   **DENNIS:** *(Grabs her arm.)* **Oh, no, no, no. I mean —** *(Singing)*

23   **Stop in the name of love, before you break my heart!** *(He*

24   *chuckles.)* **I kinda like music too.**

25   **KATHY:** *(Looking around sheepishly, asks for help.)* **Pam?!**

26   **DENNIS:** *(Looks as if he's noticed something to her right.)* **Say, uh,**

27   **I don't suppose you'd mind if I had a peanut, would you?**

28   **KATHY:** *(Pausing)* **No, no, go right ahead.**

29   **DENNIS:** **Fine.** *(Instead of reaching in front of her, he lifts his right*

30   *arm, puts it around her, reaches down and grabs an imaginary*

31   *peanut. He then puts his left arm in front of her, drops the peanut*

32   *from the right to his left hand and pops the peanut into his*

33   *mouth. With a smile, he snuggles in closer to her with his right*

34   *arm still around her. After looking around a bit, he turns toward*

35   *her, getting a whiff of her perfume. As he moves to get a closer sniff,*

1   *overplaying the sniffs, a coy smile comes across his face.)* **Say,**
2   **what's that great smell?**
3   **KATHY:** **"Passion."**
4   **DENNIS:** Let's hope so! *(Once again he chuckles at himself. JOHN*
5   *briskly enters from Stage Left and crosses behind DENNIS and*
6   *KATHY. As he does, he notices DENNIS and walks over to him.)*
7   **JOHN:** **Hey, Dennis! How ya doin'? I didn't know you were**
8   **going to be at this party.** *(DENNIS sees who is speaking and*
9   *immediately begins to get noticeably uneasy.)* **Hey, I'm glad I**
10   **ran into you. You know, you left your coat at Bible study**
11   **the other night. I've got it at my house if you want to**
12   **pick it up. Incidentally, I really appreciated what you**
13   **shared the other night about what the Lord has been**
14   **doing in your life. It really helped me. I gotta run. Take**
15   **it easy.** *(JOHN exits.)*
16   **KATHY:** **Did he say Bible study?**
17   **DENNIS:** *(By now extremely uncomfortable)* **Uh ... uh ... right. I**
18   **mean ... you know how I love literature!** *(Laughs*
19   *nervously.)*
20   **KATHY:** *(Thoughtfully)* **I knew someone like that once. He said**
21   **he was a Christian.** *(Pauses)* **He seemed so ... caring. I**
22   **sure wish I had someone like that to talk to now.** *(Pauses,*
23   *then speaks introspectively, almost trance-like.)* **You see,**
24   **it's ... uh ... it's my parents. They are ... uh ... getting**
25   **a divorce. I love them both so much.** *(DENNIS' uneasiness*
26   *and guilt increases.)* **It's hard for me to understand and to**
27   **live with the thought that my family is breaking up. I**
28   **just don't know what to do or where to turn. I was hoping**
29   **I would find someone here to talk to ... someone to offer**
30   **a little help or maybe even a little ... encouragement.**
31   *(Looking at DENNIS)* **But I guess that's not the case here.**
32   *(Pauses as guilt covers DENNIS' face.)* **I've got to go.** *(With*
33   *tears in her eyes, she quickly leaves. DENNIS makes a move to*
34   *stop her, but it's too late.)*
35   **DENNIS:** **Wait a minute, I ...** *(Looks back as if looking for*

1   *something to say to justify his actions.)* **Well, she . . . uh . . . just**
2   **didn't give me a chance.** *(Blackout)*
3
4
5
6
7
8
9
10
11
12
13
14
15
16
17
18
19
20
21
22
23
24
25
26
27
28
29
30
31
32
33
34
35

NINE

Basketball

BASKETBALL

A scene in which two Christians find out that the thrill of victory can bring a testimonial defeat.

SCENE: This sketch takes place in the bleachers at a rousing basketball game.

CHARACTERS: CAL is a very enthusiastic supporter of his team.
JEANNIE is an equally enthusiastic supporter of her team.

STAGING: The scene should be done Center Stage.

PROPS: Two folding chairs.

LIGHTING: Normal.

1   CAL: *(Yelling)* **All right, baby! Let's get up in the air and get**
2   **that ball!**
3
4   JEANNIE: *(Simultaneously with CAL)* **Come on, now, George,**
5   **take that ball away. Come on honey ... don't let him get**
6   **around ya ... stop him ... look out ... look out!**
7   CAL: **That a baby, ya got the ball now. Move it to the corner**
8   **... that a baby, drive 'round that forward ... go to the**
9   **basket ... up, up, up!**
10
11   CAL: *Two points!* **That a baby!**
12   JEANNIE: *(Mockingly)* **Two points ... that a baby!** *(Starts*
13   *yelling for her team again.)*
14
15   JEANNIE: *(Simultaneously with CAL)* **Come on, sweetie. Let's**
16   **go, honey. All right, George, pass it in ... that's it ... move**
17   **it around ... get it down to the other end ... not that**
18   **way ... watch out, watch out!**
19   CAL: **All right, now, defense, get on them tight ... watch that**
20   **pass ... force him to the side ... watch the guy in the**
21   **middle ... go for it ...**
22
23   CAL: *Good steal!*
24
25   JEANNIE: *(Simultaneously with CAL)* **What are you doin'?!**
26   *(Indiscriminate yelling and instructions continue as CAL's team*
27   *takes the ball down.)*
28   CAL: **All right, baby, go with it.** *(Indiscriminate yelling while*
29   *JEANNIE does the same.)* **Drive it up!** *Up, up!*
30
31   CAL: *Two points!* **What a slam!**
32   JEANNIE: *(Looks at CAL disgustedly, mockingly and says:)* **Two**
33   **points ... what a slam!**
34
35   JEANNIE: *(Simultaneouly with CAL)* **Come on, sweetie! Let's**

1   **try it again! Come on, now, Sugar Bear, whip that ball**
2   **around ... bring it down ... over the big dude ... one on**
3   **one ...** *drive it!*
4   **CAL:**   **All right, strong defense ... hang tight on 'em ... don't**
5   **let him get around ya ... watch that pass ... stop him.**
6   *Stop him!*
7
8   **JEANNIE:**   *Two points!* **Way to go, Sugar Bear!**
9   **CAL:**   *(Looks at JEANNIE disgustedly.)* **All right, guys, let's**
10   **double team Sugar Bear.**
11
12   **JEANNIE:**   *(Simultaneously with CAL)* **Let's go, now, George ...**
13   **watch him, Sugar Bear ... that's it ... go for the**
14   **ball ... watch the elbow ... don't let him do that!**
15   **CAL:**   **Come on, now, drive in ... dribble it down ... that's it**
16   **... look out, he's trying to steal the ball ...**
17
18   **CAL:**   **Hey, he knocked him down!**
19   **JEANNIE:**   *(Pauses)* **Stomp his eyes out, baby! Make his nose**
20   *bleeeed.*
21   **CAL:**   *(Unbelievably upset)* **Couldn't you see that, ref? He was**
22   **all over him! What are you, blind or something? Idiot!**
23   **Who's paying you anyway?**
24   **JEANNIE:**   **We are honey!** *(Pauses for a brief eye contact*
25   *confrontation with CAL.)* **Hey, we got it again! There you**
26   **go, George!** *(She energetically stands and begins to swing her*
27   *hips back and forth as she yells.)* **Look at Sugar Bear**
28   **go ... that a baby!**
29
30   **JEANNIE:**   *(Simultaneously with CAL)* **Swing it around ... put**
31   **it up ... there you go, George ...**
32   **CAL:**   **Hey, stop him! Don't let him get around you ... what**
33   **are you doing? Stop him.** *Stop him!*
34
35   **JEANNIE:**   *Two Points! (As she says "two points," she swings her*

1   *hips into CAL, knocking him to the ground. Continuing high,*
2   *gloating energy)* **Nice swish shot!** *(CAL starts to pick himself*
3   *up, and as he does so, JEANNIE continues in excitement to swing*
4   *her hips back and forth. This continues in front of him as he sits*
5   *down, obviously blocking his vision. He keeps trying to look*
6   *around her posterior until he can take it no longer.)*
7   **CAL:**   *(Stands and pushes her.)* **Would you get out of my way?**
8   **JEANNIE:**   **Would you please stop pushing me around? I'm**
9   **trying to watch a decent basketball game and you start**
10   **pushing . . .**
11   **CAL:**   **You're trying to watch the game?! I'm trying to watch**
12   **the game and you're standing here going** *(Exaggerated*
13   *copying of JEANNIE's hip movements)* **boom, boom, boom.**
14
15   **CAL:**   *(Simultaneously with JEANNIE)* **And I can't even see**
16   **what's going on! Not only that, but you're making me**
17   **look like an idiot in front of my entire** *(Loudly)* **church**
18   **singles** *(Or youth)* **group!**
19   **JEANNIE:**   **Oh, look at you! You ought to be ashamed of**
20   **yourself. Standing there doing that . . . me make you look**
21   **like an idiot? Why, you already look . . .** *(Stops dead in her*
22   *tracks realizing what he just said.)*
23
24   **JEANNIE:**   *(Laughs nervously.)* **Your church singles** *(Youth)*
25   **group?**
26   **CAL:**   *(Stares her right in the eye.)* **You got it, friend. I came to**
27   **this basketball game with my church singles** *(Youth)*
28   **group.**
29   **JEANNIE:**   *(Laughs nervously again.)* **Then you're a . . . uh . . .**
30   *(Stammering)* **a Christian!**
31   **CAL:**   *(Speaks through gritted teeth.)* **That's right . . . I am a**
32   **Christian!**
33   **JEANNIE:**   *(Laughs nervously.)* **So am I!** *(After JEANNIE says "so*
34   *am I," CAL stops and realizes what she just said. As he does,*
35   *his facial and body muscles that were tight from anger suddenly*

1   *relax and a small smile crosses his face.)*
2   **CAL: Oh ... well, praise the Lord! Um ... how's it going?**
3   **JEANNIE: Just great! You know, the Lord has really changed**
4   **my life.** *(Lights fade to black as they share small talk as if*
5   *nothing had happened and they had been friends for years.)*
6
7
8
9
10
11
12
13
14
15
16
17
18
19
20
21
22
23
24
25
26
27
28
29
30
31
32
33
34
35

TEN

A Typical Drive to Work?

A TYPICAL DRIVE TO WORK?
by PHIL LOLLAR

A look at saying one thing and doing another.

SCENE: Takes place in an automobile (chair).

CHARACTERS: DEE-JAY is a loud, energetic radio per-
                  sonality.
                  MAN is a Christian with a dual personal-
                  ity.

STAGING: Simple, Center Stage, single chair.

PROPS: Perhaps a hat.

LIGHTING: Slow fade into sketch and slow fade at
                  end. Normal spot.

SOUND EFFECTS: Car crash.

1   *AT RISE:*   The stage is dark. Out of the darkness, the sound of a
2   Robin Williams-type dee-jay fills the air. During the monolog,
3   the lights slowly rise to reveal a MAN sitting in a chair, Center
4   Stage. He pantomimes driving throughout the sketch.
5

6   **DEE-JAY: Gooooood Mooorrrning Big City! This is I. B.**
7   **Leave with the I. B. Leave Show here on the big KROS**
8   **at 77x7 on your FM dial. I'll be with you for the next four**
9   **hours, playin' the best in Christian music for your drive**
10   **to work and your morning at the office. Hey, we've got**
11   **some great tunes comin' up this hour from artists like**
12   **Sandi Patti-cake, Glen Allen, Steve Keith Green, Petra-**
13   **fied, the new a capella group, Take My Wife's Peas, and**
14   **coming up a little later, I'll spin for you the latest hit**
15   **from Grammy Ant — and I. B. Leave she's gonna win**
16   **another Grammy for this one! It's off the "Heart in**
17   **Motion, Going Straight Ahead and Never Alone from Age**
18   **to Age" album and the song is called "In a Little While**
19   **I'll Be So Glad I'm Walking Away with You on the**
20   **Mountain Top 'Cause Look What a Difference You've**
21   **Made Since Love Has Come to Our Tennessee Christmas!"**
22   **But, to get the day started off right, here's a local group:**
23   **It's** *(Insert the name of your church PIANIST/ORGANIST here)*
24   **with a new arrangement of that old favorite, "Lord, I**
25   **Want to Be a Christian."***
26   *(At this point, the PIANIST/ORGANIST should begin "Lord, I*
27   *Want to Be a Christian." The driver is pleased with this. He*
28   *hums along with the intro, then starts singing along with the*
29   *opening verses.)*
30   **MAN: That's nice . . . I like this song . . .** *(Sings)* **Lord, I want**
31   **to be a Christian . . .** *(Suddenly, he screams out the window.)*
32   **Hey, you bum! Whadda ya mean, trying to cut me off?!**
33   **Learn how to drive!** *(A beat, and he goes back to singing.)* **In**
34   **my heart, in my heart . . .** *(Again, very suddenly, he screams*
35   *out the window.)* **Where's the fire, jerk?!** *(To himself)* **Moron . . .**

1   *(Shakes his head in disgust, then starts singing again.)* **Lord,**
2   **I want to be a Christian in my heart.** *(Looks in his rear view*
3   *mirror and yells.)* **Aw, you maniac! Lay off the horn, will**
4   **ya?! Sheesh!** *(And back to singing)* **In my heart,** *(Screams)*
5   **Cork-brain!** *(Sings)* **In my heart,** *(Screams)* **You simple-**
6   **minded gherkin! Where'd you get your license — a box**
7   **of Cracker Jacks?!** *(Sings)* **Lord, I want to be a Christian**
8   *(Big finish)* **in my heart —! Aaahhh!** *(He screams and lurches*
9   *forward — and there's the sound of a crash.)*
10   **Aaagghh! Great! Just great!** *(Opens the door, storms*
11   *out — madder than ever — and starts screaming at the person*
12   *he just ran into.)* **What is the matter with you, you idiot!**
13   **Stopping in the middle of the freeway?! Are you some**
14   **kind of big dope or what? Don't act like it was my fault!**
15   **I'm gonna sue you for everything you've got . . .** *(He*
16   *continues ad-libbing in this fashion as he walks Off-stage Left.*
17   *Meanwhile, the song ends, and we hear the DEE-JAY again.)*
18   **DEE-JAY:**   **Ah, yes . . . a great message — one I know you're**
19   **taking to heart . . .**
20   *(The lights slowly fade to blackout.)*
21
22
23
24
25
26
27
28
29
30
31
32
33
34
35   **"Lord, I Want to Be a Christian," American folk hymn. May be found in*
  many hymnals and songbooks, including The Book of Hymns *(Methodist).*

ELEVEN

Sneak Previews

SNEAK PREVIEWS
by PHIL LOLLAR

A spoof of some very famous critics who ask: "Does what we see really affect us?"

SCENE:	Takes place in a studio made up to look like the balcony in a movie theatre.
CHARACTERS:	ROGER ECLAIR is a heavy-set character who wears glasses. GENE SPLEEN is a thin and balding character in a sweater.
STAGING:	Two chairs Center Stage.
PROPS:	Pencils, note cards, toy gun, shoulder holster.
LIGHTING:	Normal, with a quick blackout at the end.

1   ROGER: Welcome back to "Sneak Previews at the Movies,"
2   also known as "Two White Guys Who Sit Around and
3   Watch a Lotta Films." I'm Roger Eclair, critic for the Daily
4   Skinny . . .
5   GENE: And I'm Gene Spleen, critic for the Yellow Journal.
6   Today's topic is: "The Effect of Violence in Movies." And
7   I, for one, am really glad we're discussing this, Roger.
8   ROGER: So am I, Gene. It's about time somebody put an end
9   to this ridiculous notion that violence on the screen
10   causes violence out on the street. *(Breaks his pencil.)*
11   GENE: *(Cleaning a revolver)* You're so right, Roger. And we're
12   not just talking about physical violence, but so-called
13   "verbal violence" as well — you know: insults, put-downs,
14   that sort of thing. *(Spins the chamber on the gun and puts it*
15   *in a shoulder holster.)*
16   ROGER: Well, you know this whole argument comes from
17   the place where most misguided concepts come from —
18   the Bible. Some antiquated idea about bad company
19   corrupting good morals. I mean, who believes that piece
20   of drivel, anyway?
21   GENE: It's hogwash, of course! It's just a well-orchestrated
22   plot by a bunch of small-minded bigots to censor what
23   we see. If you want my opinion, they all oughta be shot!
24   ROGER: Yeah, after we pull out their nose hairs one by one!
25   The idea that fantasies you watch in the movies can
26   somehow affect your behavior in daily life is ludicrous
27   at best. I mean, look at me! I watch these so-called
28   "violent" films all the time, and I can hardly be called
29   violent.
30   GENE: That's for sure. In fact, in the shape you're in, you can
31   hardly be called "active!" *(A beat)*
32   ROGER: Is that supposed to be some sorta crack about my
33   weight?
34   GENE: Well, it didn't start out that way, but if the clothes fit
35   — or in your case, don't fit . . .

1   ROGER: Yeah? Well, at least I don't have to tie a string
2   around my forehead to know when to quit washing my
3   face!
4   GENE: So it's bald jokes, now, huh?
5   ROGER: No, Gene, you gots lots of hair. Too bad it's all in
6   your ears.
7   GENE: Well, you're not exactly built like Sylvester Stallone,
8   you know?
9   ROGER: *(Getting angrier)* **And you're no Schwarzenegger,**
10   Toothpick! You'd make a great pool cue if we could only
11   chalk your head!
12   GENE: Oh yeah? Well, what does it feel like to make the
13   Pillsbury Dough Boy look like an anorexic gnat? Better
14   hope no one pokes you in the stomach with their finger . . .
15   they'd drown in gravy!
16   ROGER: Now there's an intelligent statement! Now I know
17   why you don't have hair — it was offended by your face
18   and asked for a divorce!
19   GENE: *(Livid)* Ooo, if I wasn't a pacifist, I'd knock your block
20   off!
21   ROGER: Oh yeah? Well, go ahead, make my day! *(GENE lunges*
22   *at ROGER, and they start wrestling as the lights quickly fade to*
23   *black.)*
24
25
26
27
28
29
30
31
32
33
34
35

TWELVE

In the Sanhedrin Waiting Room

IN THE SANHEDRIN WAITING ROOM
by PHIL LOLLAR

A sketch that looks at our own self-importance vs. God's grace in our lives.

SCENE: Takes place in a typical waiting room environment.

CHARACTERS: RECEPTIONIST is a typical abrasive receptionist, who is not very friendly and very suspicious.
MAN is a sincere believer who is excited about being healed.
BLIND MAN 1, BLIND MAN 2, and BLIND MAN 3 are men more interested in their own importance than in God's miracle.

STAGING and
COSTUMES: A typical waiting room with sofa and coffee table Center Stage, a table and chair Stage Right, and the reception desk Stage Left. RECEPTIONIST and three MEN on stage when the lights come up, are dressed in biblical-era costumes: Long robes and cloaks, turbans, sandals — the very latest in New Testament fashions. One gent sits on the Stage Right end of the sofa reading a papyrus newspaper (if you can make one). The second sits in the center of the sofa, tapping his foot and humming along with the Middle Eastern muzak (if you can get it). The third is checking the contents of his coin purse.

PROPS: Sofa, coffee table, two tables, two chairs, papyrus newspaper (if possible), Middle Eastern muzak (if possible), coin purse, telephone, papers, pen.

LIGHTING: Normal with slow blackout at the end.

1   *AT RISE:*   The telephone rings and the RECEPTIONIST answers it.

2

3   RECEPTIONIST: *(Answering)* **Shalom! Office of the Sanhedrin,**

4   **Mary speaking ... Rabbi Caiaphas? No, I'm sorry, he's**

5   **not taking any calls today ...** *(She looks up as a young MAN*

6   *enters from Stage Right.)* **No, I'm afraid none of the rabbis**

7   **are — they're only seeing people in person ... uh-huh,**

8   **thank you.** *(She hangs up and the young MAN walks up to her.)*

9   MAN: **Excuse me, Miss.**

10   RECEPTIONIST: **Yes?**

11   MAN: **I was wondering if I could see the Sanhedrin.**

12   RECEPTIONIST: **Well, they're very busy. They're with**

13   **someone right now — I don't know how long it'll take —**

14   **and these three gentlemen are ahead of you.**

15   MAN: **I'd still like to see them. I sort of have to ... see, I was**

16   *sent* **here.**

17   RECEPTIONIST: **By who?**

18   MAN: *(Pleased)* **The Messiah.**

19   RECEPTIONIST: *(Rolling her eyes)* **Uh-huh ...**

20   MAN: **No, really! I've seen him.**

21   RECEPTIONIST: *(Ever so sweetly)* **Well, then, you're in good**

22   **company ...** *(She motions toward the others.)*

23   MAN: **You mean they —?**

24   RECEPTIONIST: *(Nodding)* **Mm-hmm.**

25   MAN: **Oh ...** *(Almost pleading)* **Well, this is kind of special.**

26   **See ... I was healed.**

27   RECEPTIONIST: *(Flatly)* **You're still in good company ...**

28   MAN: *(Can't believe it)* **No!** *(She smiles and nods.)* **Well ... I still**

29   **want to see them.**

30   RECEPTIONIST: *(Sighs impatiently)* **Oh, all right ...** *(She pulls*

31   *out a scroll and hands it to him.)* **Fill out this form and wait**

32   **with the others. I'll let the rabbis know you're here.** *(She*

33   *rises and exits Stage Left.)*

34   MAN: **Thank you.** *(He takes the scroll, moves over to the lounge*

35   *area, sits on the Stage Left end of the sofa, and starts filling out*

1   *the form. The PAPYRUS READER and COIN CHECKER*
2   *ignore him, but the FOOT TAPPER in the center watches him*
3   *curiously for a few seconds. Finally, he leans forward and taps*
4   *the MAN on the shoulder.)*
5   **BLIND MAN 1:   Uh, pardon me — I couldn't help overhearing**
6   **your conversation with the receptionist. You say you've**
7   **seen the Messiah?**
8   **MAN: Yes.**
9   **BLIND MAN 1:   And he healed you?**
10   **MAN: That's right.**
11   **BLIND MAN 1:   Oh . . .** *(A slight pause)* **Well, if it's not too much**
12   **trouble, would you mind telling me just . . . well . . . how?**
13   *(The COIN CHECKER is listening now.)*
14   **MAN:** *(Happily)* **Oh, no, I don't mind at all! See, ever since I**
15   **was small, I had a problem walking. No one knew why,**
16   **I just did. Every day, my mother and father would take**
17   **me to the pool of Bethesda — that's where I'm from —**
18   **because the story says that at certain times an angel stirs**
19   **up the water in the pool, and the first one in afterwards**
20   **is healed of whatever disease or sickness he has. Well,**
21   **anyway, one day, I was standing there on my crutches**
22   **when the Messiah and his disciples walked up. I**
23   **remember thinking how calm he seemed. Everyone knew**
24   **who he was right away, and they all gathered around**
25   **him — with all those people there, I didn't think he'd ever**
26   **notice me. But, he did! He turned and looked right at**
27   **me — and then he motioned for me to come to him! Well,**
28   **I don't have to tell you how scared I was — so I shook my**
29   **head no. But that didn't stop the Messiah. He said, "Put**
30   **down your crutches and come to me." So I slowly laid**
31   **down my crutches . . . and then took a step forward —**
32   **and I didn't fall! And with the next step, I felt my legs**
33   **grow stronger . . . and stronger . . . until I finally *ran* to**
34   **him! He hugged me and . . .** *(Composes himself)* **. . . well . . . it**
35   **was wonderful . . .** *(A beat)*

1 BLIND MAN 1:   *(With false enthusiasm)* Ah ... yes ... wonderful ...
2 MAN: You sound like you don't believe me.
3 BLIND MAN 1:   Oh, no, no — I do. I mean, I'm sure it was
4   wonderful in a ... small sort of way, but what the Messiah
5   did for me, now that was *really* wonderful! *(With great*
6   *importance)* You see, he gave me back my sight — *(The*
7   *COIN CHECKER hops in.)*
8 BLIND MAN 2:   Wait a minute! Wait a minute! He gave *you*
9   back your sight?
10 BLIND MAN 1:   That's right, on his way out to the Mount of
11   Olives.
12 BLIND MAN 2:   Well, that's interesting, 'cause *I'm* the one he
13   gave sight to!
14 BLIND MAN 1:   What?!
15 MAN: Really?
16 BLIND MAN 2:   Yeah — and it wasn't on the road to the
17   Mount of Olives, it was in Jersualem!
18 BLIND MAN 1:   Jerusalem?!
19 BLIND MAN 2:   That's right — Jerusalem! I was standing by
20   the side of the road and as Jesus passed, I cried out,
21   "Have mercy on me, Son of David! Have mercy —" *(The*
22   *PAPYRUS READER cuts in from behind his paper.)*
23 BLIND MAN 3:   *(Lowering the papyrus)* Hold it, time out,
24   everybody outta the pool. Whaddya tryin' to do — pad
25   yer part?
26 BLIND MAN 2:   I beg your pardon —
27 BLIND MAN 3:   I was the one who said, "Have mercy on me,
28   Son of David!" Me — Bartimaeus, son of Timaeus! In fact,
29   I made up that line! It came to me as Jesus was passing
30   by on the road to Jericho —
31 BLIND MAN 1:   Jericho?!
32 BLIND MAN 2:   Why in the world would he be going to
33   Jericho?
34 BLIND MAN 1:   He wouldn't! The whole thing is ridiculous!
35 BLIND MAN 3:   Izzat so? All right then, Mr. Mount of Olives,

– 91 –

1   why don't you just tell us how you think it happened?

2   BLIND MAN 1:   With pleasure! Like I said, I was sitting on my

3   usual spot on the road out to the Mount of Olives, when

4   suddenly I hears this group of men come up. And one of

5   'em sez, "Rabbi, who sinned, this man or his parents, that

6   he should be born blind?" Well, naturally, I figgers they're

7   talkin' about me, so I really listen in. And I hears the

8   Messiah say, "It wasn't that this man or his folks sinned,

9   but that the works of God might be revealed in him."

10   After that, I hears Jesus spit on the ground, and the next

11   thing I know, he's puttin' some sorta mud on my eyes.

12   Then he tells me, "Go and wash in the pool of Siloam."

13   So I did — and, lo and behold, I could see! Whaddya

14   thinka that?

15   BLIND MAN 2:   I think you musta been a real hard case if he

16   had to put mud on your eyes and make you go wash it

17   off before you could see!

18   BLIND MAN 1:   He didn't make mud for you?

19   BLIND MAN 2:   Certainly not! Some of us have a little more

20   faith than that!

21   BLIND MAN 1:   All right then, you're so pious, let's hear how

22   you think it happened to you.

23   BLIND MAN 2:   Well, I caught the Messiah just as he was

24   leaving Jairus's house — you know, the high official.

25   There were a lot of people around him then, not just his

26   disciples. And I cried out, "Have mercy on me, Son of

27   David!" Well, he musta heard me, 'cause he came over

28   and said, "Do you believe I'm able to do this?" And I said,

29   "Yes, Lord!" And he said, "Let it be done according to

30   your faith." And he simply touched my eyes — no spitting

31   or mud or washing — and I could see . . . and that's how

32   it happened. *(A pause. BLIND MAN 2 is obviously very pleased*

33   *with himself. Then:)*

34   BLIND MAN 3:   *(Very cocky)* He had to *touch* you?

35   BLIND MAN 2:   *(Shocked)* What?!

1   **BLIND MAN 1:**   **Oh, come off it! You mean to say he healed**
2   **you without touching you?**
3   **BLIND MAN 3:**   **That's exactly what I'm saying!**
4   **MAN:**   *(Awed)* **Wow ...**
5   **BLIND MAN 2:**   **Oh brother ...**
6   **BLIND MAN 3:**   **It was on the road to Jericho. And a whole**
7   **mob of people passed by, crowding around the Messiah.**
8   **And that's when the words just flew out of my mouth. I**
9   **yelled out, "Son of David, have mercy on me!" Well, I**
10   **guess the crowd didn't like it, 'cause some of them turned**
11   **around and told me to keep quiet. But that didn't stop**
12   **me, no sir! We Timaeuses are made of sterner stuff! I just**
13   **cried out all the louder, "Son of David, have mercy on**
14   **me!" Well, it worked, 'cause the Messiah stopped and told**
15   **a coupla guys to bring me to him! And the crowd was**
16   **singing a different tune after that, let me tell you! As I**
17   **passed by, I heard them say, "Have courage! He's calling**
18   **for you!" Well, when I got to him, he asked me, "What do**
19   **you want me to do for you?" And I said, "Master, I want**
20   **my sight!" And he simply said, "Go your way; your faith**
21   **has made you well." And right then, I could see! No**
22   **spitting, no mud, no washing, and no touching — just one**
23   **little sentence. Whaddya think of them olives?** *(A beat as*
24   *the young MAN looks at their faces, then:)*
25   **BLIND MAN 2:**   **You really expect us to believe that?**
26   **BLIND MAN 3:**   *(Surprised)* **Well, yes!**
27   **BLIND MAN 1:**   **That's the most far-fetched thing I've ever**
28   **heard!** *(The three of them start arguing quite loudly. This goes*
29   *on for a few seconds, then the MAN stops it.)*
30   **MAN:**   *(Above the argument)* **Stop it! Stop it! Stop it!** *(They*
31   *finally do.)* **You should all be ashamed of yourselves,**
32   **arguing over which story is true and which is false! Hasn't**
33   **it occurred to you that the Messiah is powerful enough**
34   **to give sight to all three of you?**
35   **ALL BLIND MEN:**   *(Together: puzzled)* **All three?**

1   **MAN: Yes! He is the Great Physician. He can heal any**
2   **disease — whether it be of body, mind, or heart! His is**
3   **the power of ultimate sacrifice, ultimate mercy, ultimate**
4   **love!** *(A long beat. The three MEN look at each other for a*
5   *moment, then BLIND MAN 3 turns to the young MAN.)*
6   **BLIND MAN 3:** *(Suddenly defensive)* **Whadda you know?**
7   **BLIND MAN 2: Yeah! You're just a kid got dipped in a pool!**
8   **BLIND MAN 1: Probably dipped in upside-down one too**
9   **many times . . .**
10   **BLIND MAN 3: Look, Sonny, I'm the original healed blind**
11   **man here! These other guys are just trying to horn in on**
12   **my glory!**
13   **MAN: But —**
14   **BLIND MAN 2: "Original?!" Ha! You guys wouldn't know a**
15   **healed blind man if you saw one!**
16   **MAN: Wait —**
17   **BLIND MAN 1: Well, I know I'm not looking at one when I**
18   **look at you two!**
19   **MAN: Guys —**
20   **BLIND MAN 3: Oh, yeah? Well, let's go back to Jericho and**
21   **I'll prove it!** *(He and the other BLIND MEN start Off-stage*
22   *right.)*
23   **BLIND MAN 2: I've gotta better idea — let's find the Messiah!**
24   **He'll tell you it was me!**
25   **BLIND MAN 1: Not if I get there first!** *(They all take off running*
26   *and exit Stage Right.)*
27   **MAN:** *(Calling after them)* **Uh, guys? Wait! That's not what**
28   **the Messiah told us to do! What about the Sanhedrin —?!**
29   *(But they're gone. There's a beat, and the RECEPTIONIST*
30   *enters.)*
31   **RECEPTIONIST:** *(Coming in)* **All right, the rabbis will see**
32   **you now —** *(She stops.)*
33   **MAN:** *(Turns to her.)* **Oh, uh, thank you very much . . .** *(Starts*
34   *off right.)*
35   **RECEPTIONIST: Um . . . what happened to the others?**

1   **MAN:** *(Sadly)* **They left.**
2   **RECEPTIONIST:** *(Skeptically)* **Uh-huh — I thought so! They**
3   **didn't really receive their sight, did they?**
4   **MAN:** **Oh, they received their sight, all right — but they still**
5   **can't see . . .** *(They both exit Stage Right, as the lights slowly*
6   *fade to blackout.)*
7
8
9
10
11
12
13
14
15
16
17
18
19
20
21
22
23
24
25
26
27
28
29
30
31
32
33
34
35

THIRTEEN

Not a Leg to Stand On

NOT A LEG TO STAND ON
by BOB HOOSE

A close look at how people might have approached helping one another if they had committees back in the days when Jesus walked among us.

SCENE: Takes place in a committee meeting 2,000 years ago.

CHARACTERS: MARCUS is the leader of the committee who wants to find a diplomatic solution to their problem.
JONAS is the man who pursues the best for the one in need but doesn't have the grit to do it alone.
ZEBULON is the time conscious man who needs to stick to a schedule.
JOHN is the man who recognizes the truth and follows it regardless of the cost.
SIMON is the man in need.

STAGING: First four characters are deep in discussion at one side of the stage while SIMON sits on the opposite side. JOHN enters from the same side that SIMON sits on and the others never see him.

PROPS: None needed.

LIGHTING: Regular wash with possible spots on two halves of stage if desired.

1   MARCUS: All right, all right! Let's pull this meeting
2   together now. As you all know, this committee was
3   gathered to work out the details of getting Simon here
4   to the rabbi Jesus.
5   ELI: Yes ... I've been asking this all along and I would
6   appreciate very much your telling me, how are we
7   supposed to get him there? None of us owns a donkey,
8   though if God were to give me one, I would be happy to
9   receive it.
10   JONAS: I think the Scriptures plainly say that we should go
11   the extra mile for our afflicted brother, even if it means
12   we carry him.
13   ELI: A mile for my brother, I would go. Six miles, I stay home.
14   MARCUS: OK, OK! I think we could devise some means of
15   transportation for Simon, like a stretcher or something.
16   We could take turns carrying, maybe even create a
17   schedule so we can all carry the same length of time.
18   ZEBULON: Speaking of schedules, when are we going to be
19   making this trip? I clean the stables and my boss raises
20   a real stink when I let my work pile up.
21   ELI: Right, when? *(All of the committee members start to talk at*
22   *once. ELI speaks above the other voices.)* And another
23   thing ... who's paying for lunch?
24   MARCUS: Wait! Wait! Let's put scheduling on the agenda for
25   later. There's a problem I think we should address before
26   we go any further ... the crowd.
27   JONAS: Crowd?
28   MARCUS: Of course. The rabbi Jesus is so popular nowadays
29   that the place will be swamped as soon as the word gets
30   out. So, how do we get Simon in to see him?
31   ELI: Perhaps we could book him here at the local synagogue.
32   We could even sell tickets. Not that I would want to
33   appear greedy, but it couldn't hurt.
34   ZEBULON: Couldn't we just make an appointment?
35   JONAS: He doesn't keep a calendar — it's first come, first served.

1   So as I see it, after we get Simon there we only have one
2   way to get him in to see Jesus.
3   ELI: What's that?
4   JONAS: Tunnel. We've got to dig under the hut. And with
5   about sixty men we could . . .
6   ZEBULON: *(Interrupts)* No. There's got to be an easier way!
7   What about the roof?
8   MARCUS: Yes! We could cut a hole and lower him down.
9   ELI: Hold it! . . . May God cause my wife to grow a nose like
10   yours if I am anything but wholly committed to my
11   brother . . . but! . . . do you know what it costs to repair a
12   roof these days? Not to mention the price of rope which
13   is like gold. I'm afraid the synagogue financial committee
14   won't support this.
15   ZEBULON: Maybe we should form a rope committee. *(All
16   begin to talk again. Near SIMON a man walks Onstage.
17   COMMITTEE freezes.)*
18   JOHN: *(To SIMON)* Wonderful day, isn't it?
19   SIMON: I suppose.
20   JOHN: I'm going to see the rabbi Jesus in the town of
21   Capernaum. Walk with me.
22   SIMON: I can't. My legs have been crippled since childhood.
23   JOHN: Then you must come with me. I've heard that this man
24   is the Messiah. He can heal the lame and give you back
25   your strength.
26   SIMON: *(Looks over to the committee.)* But I can't. *(JOHN begins
27   to lift him.)* You'll carry me?
28   JOHN: God has given me life and health. The least I can give
29   you is the strength of my back. *(JOHN carries SIMON Off-
30   stage. COMMITTEE comes alive again but never notices SIMON
31   is gone.)*
32   MARCUS: Perhaps what we need is a consultant to come in
33   and show us how to work this out. *(Begins to exit, others follow.)*
34   This isn't my job, you know — the synagogue asked me
35   to do this . . . *(Animated discussion begins as they exit.)*

FOURTEEN

Stress

STRESS
by PHIL LOLLAR

A sketch that examines the consequences of ignoring the cancer of the 90's.

SCENE:	Takes place in JIM's apartment.
CHARACTERS:	JIM is a hard-working citizen unaware that he is under incredible stress. DR. BART MEEDLEMEYER is a TV psychiatrist a la Sigmund Freud.
STAGING:	May be performed two ways: 1. You can stage everything Center Stage with DR. MEEDLEMEYER pre-recorded on video and shown on the TV, or 2. Build a set Stage Left with DR. MEEDLEMEYER doing his lines from there with a video camera broadcasting the scene to JIM's TV.
PROPS:	Briefcase with papers inside, TV and remote control, couch, phone.
LIGHTING:	Normal, with a blackout at the end.
SOUND EFFECTS:	Taped theme music for show.

1   *AT RISE:*   The lights rise on JIM's apartment. There's a sofa center,
2   a table at one end with a telephone on it, and a TV on a stand
3   in front of it. The place is empty, but after a few seconds, JIM
4   walks in from a long day at work, looking like something the
5   cat just dragged in. He mutters to himself.
6

7   **JIM:**   **Boy oh boy oh boy oh boy oh boy** ... *(He drops his*
8   *briefcase on the floor and plops onto the sofa.)* **What a day. I'm**
9   **bushed ... bushed, bushed, bushed, bushed, bushed** ...
10   **President Bush couldn't be more bushed than I am. I'm**
11   **so bushed I may turn into a tree. Maybe I'll turn on the**
12   **TV instead.** *(He switches on the tube. There is a brief music*
13   *theme, during which an announcer is heard.)*
14   **ANNOUNCER:**   **And now with your Mental Health Minute,**
15   **here's Dr. Bart Meedlemeyer!**
16   **JIM:**   *(To himself)* **Oh, great ... just what we need ... another**
17   **TV quack head shrink** ...
18   **DOCTOR:**   **Hello out there! And good mental health to you!**
19   **Today, we want to talk about a growing problem in the**
20   **United States:** *stress.*
21   **JIM:**   *(Snide)* **Stress ... ooo, how original.**
22   **DOCTOR:**   **You know, these days, when a big storm**
23   **approaches, hardly anybody gets hurt because we have**
24   **all sorts of warnings about it. Well, stress is no different!**
25   **JIM:**   **What a load of hooey** ... *(From this point on, JIM stops*
26   *listening to what is said on the television. He wanders around,*
27   *acting out all of the symptoms of extreme stress just prior to DR.*
28   *MEEDLEMEYER explaining them.)*
29   **DOCTOR:**   **That's right! There are definite warning signs a**
30   **person experiences when he is under too much stress.**
31   **The first one would have to be** ...
32   **JIM:**   *(Stretches and yawns.)* **Oh, man, am I tired.**
33   **DOCTOR:**   ... **exhaustion. A general feeling of tiredness** ...
34   **a loss of energy** ...
35   **JIM:**   **I really should call Rita tonight.**

1   **DOCTOR:** ... a difficulty keeping up ...

2   **JIM:** I haven't talked to her all week.

3   **DOCTOR:** This exhaustion usually leads to ...

4   **JIM:** *(Pained)* **Aw, I don't wanna talk to her.**

5   **DOCTOR:** ... detachment. That is, distancing one's self from

6   others — especially those closest to us.

7   **JIM:** Well, she is my girlfriend ... *(He picks up the phone*

8   *begrudgingly and dials.)*

9   **DOCTOR:** Victims of extreme stress have neither the time

10   nor the energy to properly pursue, build and nurture

11   relationships.

12   **JIM:** *(Unexcited)* **Hello, Rita? It's Jim.**

13   **DOCTOR:** All of their time and strength is spent just trying

14   to keep their heads above water.

15   **JIM:** *(Blasé)* **Nothing's wrong, I'm just tired from work, that's**

16   **all.**

17   **DOCTOR:** Of course, detachment always leads to the next

18   step ...

19   **JIM:** *(Extremely bored; a huge sigh)* **Yes, Rita, I know you have**

20   **lots of cures for tiredness.**

21   **DOCTOR:** ... boredom ...

22   **JIM:** *(Very bored)* **I've heard them all ... oh, you've got a new**

23   **one?**

24   **DOCTOR:** ... the sensation that nothing is new or fresh, and

25   the feeling that nothing ever will be again. Once boredom

26   sets in, it's only a short hop to its natural companion ...

27   **JIM:** *(Very cynical)* **Oh, right, Rita ... I'm so sure.**

28   **DOCTOR:** ... cynicism. One fathers the other, and they both

29   feed off each other, until finally ...

30   **JIM:** *(Impatiently)* **Yes, yes, yes ... I understand that part,**

31   **Rita! Get on with it.**

32   **DOCTOR:** ... the victim becomes impatient with those

33   around him, and that soon leads to ...

34   **JIM:** *(Irritably)* **Rita ... get on with it!**

35   **DOCTOR:** ... extreme irritability. As stress takes hold ...

1   JIM: That's the dumbest thing I've ever heard! What are you
2   talking about?
3   DOCTOR: ... impatience grows and flare-ups occur.
4   JIM: *(Cutting)* Oh, really? Well listen, it's not my fault this
5   thing isn't working out.
6   DOCTOR: They blame those closest to them for things that
7   are their own fault ...
8   JIM: All right, all right ... fine! If that's the way you want it,
9   fine! *(He slams down the receiver.)*
10   DOCTOR: ... resulting in a breaking off of the relationship.
11   JIM: *(Heavy sigh)* Well, it looks like the private life is in the
12   toilet. *(He sits for a second.)*
13   DOCTOR: Of course, these are just the preliminary
14   symptoms. *(JIM picks up his briefcase and starts taking papers*
15   *out of it.)*
16   JIM: Oh, well, there's always work.
17   DOCTOR: Once these preliminaries take hold, they move
18   quickly to the more serious symptoms, the first one
19   being ...
20   JIM: After all, I'm the best at what I do.
21   DOCTOR: ... a feeling of omnipotence. Many stress victims
22   say to themselves ...
23   JIM: Nobody can do my job like me.
24   DOCTOR: "Nobody can do my job like me," and ...
25   JIM: In fact, I'm the only one who can do it.
26   DOCTOR: "I'm the only one who can do it." And sometimes,
27   they may even think ...
28   JIM: Not even God can do this job ...
29   DOCTOR: ... "Not even God can do this job ..."
30   JIM: ... just me ...
31   DOCTOR: "... just me." Now, while these feelings are
32   completely involuntary, it goes without saying that this
33   subliminal mindset borders on the delusional.
34   JIM: *(Suddenly stops working.)* Wait a minute ... what am I
35   doing?

1   **DOCTOR:** From here, we move on to the next sign of extreme
2   stress.
3   **JIM:** I just came off a hard day of work . . . *(He stands.)*
4   **DOCTOR:** It's a very significant sign.
5   **JIM:** Not that those slave drivers I work for care at all. *(He*
6   *begins pacing about the room.)*
7   **DOCTOR:** It's the belief that he is unappreciated. The
8   stressed out person runs through a maze of feelings.
9   **JIM:** *(Bitterly)* **Those lousy . . .**
10   **DOCTOR:** They include bitterness . . .
11   **JIM:** *(Angry)* **. . . stinking . . .**
12   **DOCTOR:** . . . anger . . .
13   **JIM:** *(Resentful)* **How dare they?!**
14   **DOCTOR:** . . . offense . . .
15   **JIM:** *(Anxious)* **Ooo, I'm so on the edge!**
16   **DOCTOR:** . . . and anxiety because he feels his work is not
17   appreciated.
18   **JIM:** *(Puts his papers back into his briefcase.)* **Well, I may have**
19   put in long hours before, but not now!
20   **DOCTOR:** This belief usually results in a deviation from his
21   normal work pattern.
22   **JIM:** If they thought I was hard to work with before, they
23   ain't seen nothin' yet!
24   **DOCTOR:** He becomes more tyrannical, demanding, and
25   inflexible . . . from here, it's a very small step to the next
26   stage's symptom . . .
27   **JIM:** They're all out to get me anyway!
28   **DOCTOR:** . . . paranoia. This, of course, is a very serious
29   condition that can have many long-term and damaging
30   side effects.
31   **JIM:** *(Suddenly confused)* **What was I thinking about?**
32   **DOCTOR:** The stress victim will become disoriented, and his
33   thought processes will wander.
34   **JIM:** I thought I had . . . I was going . . . what was the . . . when
35   I . . .

1   **DOCTOR:**   He will have increasing difficulty communicating.

2   **JIM:**   C'mon ... think, think, think ...

3   **DOCTOR:**   He will lose the ability to concentrate.

4   **JIM:**   Oh, yeah! It was about, uh, what's-her-flibber?

5   **DOCTOR:**   His memory for names, dates, and even what he
6   started to say will dwindle.

7   **JIM:**   *(Chortles to himself.)* **Huh ... guess creeping senility is**
8   **taking its toll on the ol' noodle.**

9   **DOCTOR:**   He will joke about increasing old age ... and,
10   thus, try to cover his problems further. This is a very
11   unattractive explanation for his poor performances, so
12   another reason must be found ...

13   **JIM:**   *(Stretches and suddenly looks very pained.)* **Ooww ... it's not**
14   **my mind that's falling apart ... it's my body ...**

15   **DOCTOR:**   ... physical ailments. These bodily complaints
16   can appear and flourish anywhere on the victim ...

17   **JIM:**   *(Grabs his head.)* **What a headache.**

18   **DOCTOR:**   ... the head ...

19   **JIM:**   *(Feels his back.)* **Ow ... my back's not doing too good**
20   **either ...**

21   **DOCTOR:**   ... the back ... *(JIM lets out a head-splitting sneeze.)*
22   the sinuses ... *(JIM goes completely limp and plops onto the*
23   *couch again.)* ... even the entire musculature structure.
24   *(JIM moans very loudly ... a depressed moan.)* **Although these**
25   **problems may be real, they are usually brought on by**
26   **the extreme emotional stress the person is suffering.** *(JIM*
27   *moans even deeper.)* **And of course, all of these things can**
28   **lead to one of the most devastating stages of all ...**

29   **JIM:**   *(Another moan)* **I hate my life.**

30   **DOCTOR:**   ... depression. This is the worst stage because it
31   can springboard into even more serious behavior later
32   on.

33   **JIM:**   *(Looks at the television cynically.)* **What *is* this nonsense?**

34   **DOCTOR:**   So those are just a few of the warning signs that a
35   person is suffering from extreme stress.

1   **JIM:**   *(Cynical)* **Oh, brother . . .**

2   **DOCTOR: The truly alarming thing is that most people**

3   **refuse to recognize the symptoms, even when they're**

4   **confronted with them face to face. They tend to want to**

5   **shut out any potential help. This has been Dr. Bart**

6   **Meedlemeyer with your Mental Health Minute.**

7   **JIM:**   *(Disgusted)* **Aw, get outa here!** *(He reaches out and abruptly*

8   *snaps off the TV, cutting off the doctor midsentence.)* **Just what**

9   **we need . . . another quack TV head shrink . . .** *(He rises,*

10   *drags himself Off-stage, mumbling the whole way as the lights*

11   *slowly fade to blackout.)*

12

13

14

15

16

17

18

19

20

21

22

23

24

25

26

27

28

29

30

31

32

33

34

35

FIFTEEN

Engaged

ENGAGED
by JIM CUSTER

When is a couple "married" in the eyes of God — before or after the ceremony? This sketch asks that question and more.

SCENE: This sketch takes place in an apartment at night.

CHARACTERS: TEDDY is an over-anxious young man counting the minutes 'till he hears wedding bells.
LAURA is his more sensible and patient wife to be.
BERNIE FETTERS is a man in his sixties, a comic "Newhart"-like character.
IRT is BERNIE's faithful and quiet wife.

STAGING: Basic. Should be done Center Stage with outside door either Stage Left or Right.

PROPS: The stage should look like a small apartment with a couch and chairs. If you want to go simpler, some folding chairs put together will give you the same effect.

LIGHTING: Normal, with a blackout at the end.

SOUND EFFECTS: Telephone, doorbell.

1 **AT RISE:** TEDDY and LAURA are sitting on the couch.

2

3 TEDDY: *(Looking around)* **The place looks great, Sweetie.**

4 LAURA: **Thanks. Mom and I spent the whole day putting up**

5 **wallpaper. If I ever see another blue goose . . . I'll shoot it.**

6 TEDDY: **Well, it looks very nice.**

7 LAURA: **Can you believe, Teddy, that in one week we'll be**

8 **married? No more invitations to send out, or rehearsals,**

9 **or saying goodbye at night, or . . .**

10 TEDDY: *(Interrupting)* **Or cold showers.**

11 LAURA: **It'll be you and me against the world, kiddo. Here**

12 **in our little love nest . . .** *(Phone rings.)* **Hold that thought.**

13 *(Starts to go but Teddy pulls her back.)*

14 TEDDY: **Forget the phone.**

15 LAURA: **I can't. What if it's important?**

16 TEDDY: **It's not, trust me.**

17 LAURA: **How do you know?**

18 TEDDY: **Men's intuition.**

19 LAURA: **There's no such thing.**

20 TEDDY: **There is and it's scary.**

21 LAURA: **You're scary.** *(Phone stops ringing.)* **See there, I**

22 **missed it. It could have been Ed McMahon with my ten**

23 **million.**

24 TEDDY: **Who cares? We don't need money, we've got love —**

25 **now come here and give me a kiss.** *(Puckers up.)*

26 LAURA: *(Eludes his puckered lips.)* **I know that look, Teddy,**

27 **and we've got lots of preparations for the wedding yet,**

28 **so let's not get sidetracked.**

29 TEDDY: **I know we have to get things done, but Hon, for the**

30 **past four months it's been nothing but plans, dresses,**

31 **invitations, songs, relatives, and every thing or body else.**

32 **At this point, I feel like I know the flower man better**

33 **than you. I just want a little time with you. Is that too**

34 **much to ask?**

35 LAURA: **It has been a little overwhelming, hasn't it?**

1   **TEDDY:**   Yeah, but we can slow down. It's just us, alone,
2   *(He takes her hand and pulls her onto the couch)* **in our little**
3   **love nest . . .**
4   **LAURA:**   *(Interrupting)* **But there are so many details to think**
5   **of.**
6   **TEDDY:**   *(Putting his finger to her lips)* **Shhh.** *(Just as he leans*
7   *over to kiss her, the doorbell rings. She immediately gets up and*
8   *he falls over on the couch.)* **There's got to be sin in my life.**
9   **LAURA:**   *(Answering the door)* **Hello.**
10   **BERNIE:**   Well, howdy. *(Grabs her hand and shakes vigorously.)*
11   **You're the new neighbors, huh?**
12   **LAURA:**   Yes, I'm Laura and *(Pointing to TEDDY)* **this is Teddy.**
13   *(TEDDY's head is buried in the couch. He raises his hand and*
14   *limply waves.)*
15   **BERNIE:**   He sick?
16   **LAURA:**   No, just a little exhausted planning for the wedding.
17   **BERNIE:**   Oh, I know how that is.
18   **LAURA:**   You do?
19   **BERNIE:**   No, not really, but it seemed like a good thing to
20   say. Well, we're the Fetters. I'm Bernie and this is my
21   wife Irt. *(Grabs her hand and starts to shake vigorously again.)*
22   **LAURA:**   Well, nice to meet you.
23   **BERNIE:**   Oh no, the pleasure is ours. It's good to have
24   neighbors again.
25   **LAURA:**   You haven't had any for awhile?
26   **BERNIE:**   No, not since the Pods.
27   **LAURA:**   The Pods?
28   **BERNIE:**   Yeah, Peter and his wife Patty.
29   **LAURA:**   Peter Pod and Patty Pod?
30   **IRT:**   And their two pets, Po and Pungy.
31   **LAURA:**   Po and Pungy?
32   **BERNIE:**   They were penguins.
33   **LAURA:**   You're pulling my leg, aren't you, Mr. Fetters?
34   **BERNIE:**   *(Confused)* **No, you're standing there. I'm over here.**
35   **Besides, Irt wouldn't like that. Well, listen, if there is**

1   anything we can do, just let us know. We don't have a
2   phone but we can hear real good. Just plant your feet
3   out here and yell *(Yells)* "Bernie, Irt!" We'll come running.
4   LAURA: Thanks! *(BERNIE and IRT exit. LAURA closes door and*
5   *sits back down on the couch.)* What a nice couple. Sort of
6   like *The Beverly Hillbillies*, don't you think?
7   TEDDY: Huh? *(Head still in couch)*
8   LAURA: What is the matter with you?
9   TEDDY: Oh, nothing. Nothing that a good marriage won't
10   fix. Laura, you love me, right?
11   LAURA: No, I'm gonna marry you now and love you later.
12   TEDDY: I'm being serious.
13   LAURA: Of course I love you.
14   TEDDY: Well, when you love someone you want the best for
15   them, right?
16   LAURA: Right.
17   TEDDY: And there's only one more week, right?
18   LAURA: Right.
19   TEDDY: And technically a week from right now we'll be on
20   our honeymoon, right?
21   LAURA: Right.
22   TEDDY: Did you open your presents on Christmas Eve or
23   Christmas?
24   LAURA: *(Confused)* Huh?
25   TEDDY: Answer the question.
26   LAURA: Christmas Eve.
27   TEDYD: Good, so did I. *(Starts to sing "Jingle Bells" with a smile*
28   *on his face.)*
29   LAURA: You're weird. This is not Christmas and we don't
30   have any . . . *(Dawns on her what he wants.)* Teddy, no . . . we
31   have . . .
32   TEDDY: *(Interrupts)* It is only seven days, Laura — a speck of
33   sand in eternity, a drop in the ocean of time, a small tick
34   on the big clock of life.
35   LAURA: Your clock's stopped. We promised ourselves and

1   the Lord we would wait.

2   TEDDY: I know, but I'm a forgiving kind of guy and I know
3   God is, so . . .

4   LAURA: So *what?* You're being dumb.

5   TEDDY: It comes from too many cold showers. *(Sweetly)*
6   Laura . . .

7   LAURA: *(Interrupts)* No. I can't believe we're discussing this.
8   We decided on this a long time ago! We have one more
9   week.

10   TEDDY: Laura, we have vowed our love for each other.
11   Waiting is a technicality.

12   LAURA: A technicality? If we break this vow now . . .

13   TEDDY: *(Being cute, interrupting)* Vow now brown cow.

14   LAURA: Teddy, if we break our vow now, who's to say we
15   won't break our wedding vows later? "Little foxes spoil
16   the vines."

17   TEDDY: "America, love it or leave it."

18   LAURA: What?

19   TEDDY: I don't know, I couldn't think of anything fast
20   enough. Laura, in the eyes of God we are already married.
21   I'm — I'm sure it's OK.

22   LAURA: Teddy . . .

23   TEDDY: No, listen — if I had any doubts this was wrong or
24   would jeopardize our marriage, would I ask you to do
25   this?

26   LAURA: Yes.

27   TEDDY: We love each other! In seven days, a mere 185 hours,
28   11,100 minutes, 666,000 seconds we'll be one. If we love
29   each other, the time isn't important.

30   LAURA: Teddy, if we truly love each other, then the time
31   doesn't matter — love will be there in seven days, 185
32   hours, 11,100 minutes, 666,000 seconds. We can wait.

33   TEDDY: Sounds so long.

34   LAURA: Take a cold shower.

35   TEDDY: I've taken so many my feet are starting to web.

1   LAURA: You're funny and cute.
2   TEDDY: Great, I'm funny and cute. Me and Mickey Mouse
3   should have it so lucky.
4   LAURA: Hang in there, pilgrim, we can do it! *(Gives him a short*
5   *kiss.)* There, isn't that better?
6   TEDDY: Compared to what? Are you sure there's no way?
7   LAURA: Teddy, when we stand in front of the pastor, I want
8   to stand there pure. It's important to me. Do you
9   understand?
10 TEDDY: A month ago I understood, last week I understood,
11   today I'm not so sure, but OK.
12 LAURA: I knew I could count on you. *(TEDDY starts to exit.)*
13   Where are you going?
14 TEDDY: Home. I'm gonna take my cute, funny, dependable
15   body home, and go to bed. Who knows, maybe the rapture
16   will come. With my luck, God will ask me to wait a week.
17
18
19
20
21
22
23
24
25
26
27
28
29
30
31
32
33
34
35

SIXTEEN

Car Crash

CAR CRASH

Car Crash takes place at the scene of an accident between two young married couples. In the heat of their argument over whose fault it was, they discover another "accident" they have made . . . both are on their way to church.

SCENE: This sketch takes place at the scene of a car accident (obviously). Chuck and Jeannie's car has just hit Mick and Vicki's.

CHARACTERS: MICK and VICKI are a fairly normal, young married couple. MICK is a generally non-excitable type but this accident has pushed him to the limit. VICKI is the "unable to cope" weeping type in this situation.
CHUCK and JEANNIE are an "interesting" duo. CHUCK is a very henpecked person and would probably have to gain a lot more respect and weight to dominate his wife. JEANNIE wears the pants in the family and has a tendency to come on like a marauding elephant when she is upset.

STAGING: Four chairs should be placed at about forty-five degree angles opposite from the audience. The side chairs should be no more than five feet apart. A minimum of one microphone per car should be placed between each couple. Two microphones should be placed Center Stage. Conversation begins with CHUCK and JEANNIE collecting themselves from the collision. JEANNIE then verbally assaults CHUCK.

PROPS: Four chairs, a sport hat and sunglasses for MICK and a Sunday hat for JEANNIE.

LIGHTING: Normal. Lights come up after sound of the crash. Blackout at the end.

SOUND
EFFECTS: During set-up of the sketch, while the chairs and mikes are being positioned in the dark, it might be good to have someone Off-stage making the sound of passing cars and then the crash. If no one is able to do that, you might make a recording of a crash from any typical TV action show.

1   **JEANNIE:** **I've told you a million times you drive too fast!**
2   **You were driving fifty-five miles per hour in a thirty-five**
3   **miles per hour zone. But do you listen to me? No! You**
4   **never listen to me. All I do, according to you, is nag, nag,**
5   **nag. Well, why don't you get out of the car, be a man for**
6   **once and see what's going on?** *(JEANNIE pushes him.*
7   *Cowering, CHUCK gets out and moves toward MICK who has*
8   *gotten out of his car at about the same time.)* **You big dummy!**
9   *(Under her breath)* **He never listens to me.**
10 **MICK:** *(Takes off his hat and glasses as he turns to his wife just*
11 *before stepping out.)* **If you're OK, honey, I'll be right back.**
12 **I've got to check the damages.**
13 **VICKI:** *(Shaking and sobbing)* **Oh, be careful!** *(Sobs again. MICK*
14 *inspects the damage as anger crosses his face. He approaches*
15 *CHUCK Center Stage.)*
16 **MICK:** **Nice job, Buddy ...**
17 **CHUCK:** **Yeah, I ...**
18 **MICK:** **Real nice job.**
19 **CHUCK:** **Yeah, yeah ... see ...**
20 **MICK:** **That sports cars right there** *(Pointing to his own car)* **is**
21 **only two days old. *Two days!***
22 **CHUCK:** **Right, well ...**
23 **MICK:** **We were so happy.**
24 **CHUCK:** **Uh, huh, but you ...**
25 **MICK:** **Now look at it. The bumper's all smashed in ...**
26 **headlight ... nothing left of it ... one wheel is** *(Yelling)*
27 **rolling around in the street! You *dummy!* Where did you**
28 **learn to drive? What do you think this is? Bumper cars**
29 **or something?**
30 **CHUCK:** *(Finally getting a word in)* **I'm sorry sir, but I think it**
31 **was you who ran that stop sign back there.** *(Smiling)*
32 **MICK:** *(Oblivious to what CHUCK just said)* **And my poor wife**
33 **... she's sitting back there crying ...** *(VICKI sobs loudly)*
34 **in pain, probably in shock!** *(Yelling)* **Why, I ought to punch**
35 **you right in the nose!** *(Grabs CHUCK's shirt.)*

1 **JEANNIE:** *(Jumps out of the car, jumps in between the two men*
2 *and shoves CHUCK out of the way toward their car.)* **Now wait**
3 **a minute here, Buster! Sit down, Chuckie!** *(Pauses and*
4 *stares at MICK face to face.)* **Now just who do you think you**
5 **are, getting ready to punch my husband in the nose?**
6 **MICK:** *(Backing off a bit and slightly cowering)* **Well, look what**
7 **he did to our car!**
8 **JEANNIE:** **Your car . . . well, look at our car!**
9 **MICK:** **Yeah, well that piece of junk shouldn't even be on the**
10 **road.**
11 **JEANNIE:** **Piece of junk?! Well, at least we've got four**
12 **wheels and you've only got three.**
13 **MICK:** **Yeah, since you hit us.** *(CHUCK, regaining his courage,*
14 *stands up to get back in the action. JEANNIE notices him and*
15 *shoves him back down.)*
16 **JEANNIE:** **Sit down, Chuckie!** *(Turning back to MICK)* **What do**
17 **you mean, "since we hit you"? If you had seen that stop**
18 **sign down on the corner, things would be a whole lot**
19 **better around here.**
20 **MICK:** **I don't know what you're talking about, ma'am.**
21 **JEANNIE:** **Listen, you just . . .** *(VICKI sobs loudly and stands to*
22 *get out of the car to get MICK's consoling.)* **Sit down, honey.**
23 **You ain't dead yet!** *(VICKI's sobs immediately stop in surprise*
24 *as she sits back down.)*
25 **MICK:** **You've got a lot of nerve! You cannot talk to my wife**
26 **like that!**
27 **JEANNIE:** **I just did it!** *(Pauses)* **Now, why don't you go ahead**
28 **and admit that you did not see that stop sign down there**
29 **on the corner?**
30 **MICK:** **I don't know what you're talking about. I just . . .**
31 **JEANNIE:** *(Cutting him short)* **Don't you see that red and**
32 **white sign down there? It says, S-T-O-P . . . and you didn't**
33 **do it! Now, why don't you just go ahead and admit it?**
34 **MICK:** *(He turns and looks behind him to the corner and realizes he*
35 *did, indeed, run the stop sign.)* **Gee, I sure didn't see that**

1   **thing, ma'am. I guess it really was my fault. I'm sorry.**

2 **JEANNIE:** **Well, finally! So you are admitting you ran the**

3   **sign?**

4 **MICK:** **Unfortunately, yes.**

5 **JEANNIE:** **Did you hear that Chuckie?** *(CHUCK nods.)* **And**

6   **how about you, "Niagara Falls"?** *(Speaking to VICKI. She*

7   *nods and sobs loudly.)* **Just as I thought . . . call a doctor.**

8   *(JEANNIE grabs her own neck.)*

9 **MICK:** **What do you mean? What's wrong?**

10 **CHUCK:** *(CHUCK jumps to his feet to hold her.)* **Can't you see my**

11   **wife is in pain?**

12 **MICK:** **Pain?**

13 **CHUCK:** **Yeah. It's obviously a whiplash!**

14 **MICK:** **Whiplash?**

15 **JEANNIE:** **You've got it! We're gonna sue you for everything**

16   **you've got, honey. Your house, your clothes, and even**

17   **that three-wheeled car of yours.**

18 **MICK:** *(Really shaken)* **Now . . . wa . . . wait a minute. We didn't**

19   **mean to do it. We were just on our way to church, minding**

20   **our own business and somehow I didn't . . .**

21 **CHUCK:** **Wait a minute.**

22 **CHUCK and JEANNIE:** *(In unison)* **On your way to church?**

23 **MICK:** **Yeah. I suppose we were a little late so I just . . .** *(An* ·

24   *obvious change of heart comes over JEANNIE and CHUCK's*

25   *expressions as JEANNIE stands up straight and takes her hand*

26   *away from her neck.)*

27 **CHUCK:** **Oh. well, uh . . . no problem. We . . . uh . . . were . . .**

28   **uh . . . just joking! Right, dear?** *(Turns to JEANNIE and she*

29   *agrees.)* **Yeah, we always like to keep things light in tense**

30   **situations. I mean, I think that's how the Lord would do**

31   **it, don't you, dear?** *(She nods in agreement.)* **You see, we're**

32   **Christians too . . . and believe it or not, we're on our way**

33   **to church, too!**

34 **MICK:** *(Relief and embarrassment crosses over his face.)* **Boy, you**

35   **had me worried there for a minute. I feel so foolish about the**

1   **way I acted.**

2   **CHUCK:**   **So do we. I mean, we shouldn't have lost our temper**

3   **either. Please accept our apologies.**

4   **MICK:**   **Oh, that's all right. I guess we're just human.** *(They all*

5   *laugh in relief over the past few minutes.)*

6   **CHUCK:** *(Laughter dying down)* **Yeah, hard to believe we**

7   **would act like that.** *(Pauses)* **Well, say, what** *(Insert your*

8   *denomination)* **church do you attend?**

9   **MICK:** **Oh, we aren't** *(Above denomination)*. **We go to the**

10   *(Name of another, possibly rival denomination)* **church down**

11   **the street.** *(Surprised, CHUCK and JEANNIE look at one*

12   *another and almost nod in understanding of their next action.)*

13   **JEANNIE:** *(Grabbing her neck and yelling in pain)* **Oooo! My**

14   **neck!** *(Lights fade to black as CHUCK starts rambling about*

15   *suing again. MICK looks in disbelief to the audience as an Off-*

16   *stage voice in the distance sings, "They'll Know We Are Christian*

17   *by Our Love.")*

18   *(Full blackout)*

19

20

21

22

23

24

25

26

27

28

29

30

31

32

33

34

35

SEVENTEEN

Jesus Calls

JESUS CALLS

Jesus Calls involves a conversation between a busy church secretary and a very "unexpected" visitor who wants to speak to the church people. Unfortunately, she just can't fit him into the schedule.

SCENE: This sketch takes place in the pastor's office at his secretary's desk.

CHARACTERS: SECRETARY should be a Lily Tomlin type . . . rather nasal, antsy, little odd giggles here and there, etc. Her character should be very animated.
                  VOICE OF JESUS should not be a big deep voice, but rather a nice comfortable male voice.

STAGING: SECRETARY should be seated Center Stage facing the audience. Her lines should be delivered as if Jesus was standing right in front of her.

PROPS: None necessary, although if you wish, you can set up a desk with papers and an appointment book.

LIGHTING: Normal, with a blackout at the end.

SOUND
EFFECTS: If you wish, the sketch can open with the SECRETARY miming typing with the sound of a typewriter coming from Off-stage. Also, the sound of a telephone ringing at various points in the sketch would be nice.

1   **SECRETARY:** *(Phone rings, she clears throat.)* **Good morning!**
2   **Oak Park Community Church, Miss** *(Your name)*
3   **speaking ... no, I'm sorry, the pastor's not in. May I take**
4   **a message? Oh, hi, Fern!** *(Laughs)* **Yes ... let me get my**
5   **pad ... OK, dear ...** *(Writes)* **Um-hmmm ... uh-huh ...**
6   **um-hmmm! Oh my, that is a goodie!** *(Catches herself.)* **I**
7   **mean ... I'm sure the pastor will want to make it a matter**
8   **of serious prayer ... yes, dear ... oh, goodbye.** *(Resumes*
9   *typing until the phone rings again.)* **Good morning, Oak Park**
10   **Community Church, Miss** *(Your name)* **speaking. What's**
11   **that? No, sir, the number for the "Kozy Kutie Club" is**
12   **909-5212. This is 909-5213 ... yes, I'm very sure.** *(Indignant)*
13   **No sir, this is definitely not Gloria Boom Boom! I'm Miss**
14   *(Your name)*, **the pastor's secretary.** *(Shock)* **Well, the same**
15   **to you, I'm sure!** *(Hangs up.)* **Gloria Boom Boom indeed!**
16   *(Ethereal "ooo's" sung from Off-stage [In parallel 5ths] as*
17   *invisible VISITOR enters.)* **Well, good morning, sir. May I**
18   **help you?**
19   **VISITOR:** **Good morning, my sister. Peace be with you.**
20   **SECRETARY:** **Huh?** *(Recovering)* **Oh sir, if you're looking for**
21   **... uh ... assistance, the Calvary Mission is just two**
22   **blocks down on Madison.**
23   **VISITOR:** **I didn't come to take anything from you ... I came**
24   **to give.**
25   **SECRETARY:** **Oh, I see ... sir, didn't you see the little sign**
26   **out front — "No Solicitors"? Now, if you don't mind, I'm**
27   **very busy.**
28   **VISITOR:** **No one should ever be too busy for me. I've come**
29   **to speak to your people.**
30   **SECRETARY:** **Oh, uh, sir, just what group do you represent?**
31   **VISITOR:** **I've been sent by my Father. I have a message for**
32   **them.**
33   **SECRETARY:** **Well, that's very nice, sir, but you see, we do**
34   **have a rather full schedule of events here at Oak Park.**
35   **We can't just pop things in at the last minute.**

1 VISITOR: They must hear me. My Father wants them to come
2   back to him as a holy people — totally his own. The time
3   is short.
4 SECRETARY: Well, I'm very sorry, sir, but you see, our
5   theme for this month is "God Is Great, Investigate."
6   *(Laughs)* Now, I don't quite see how your subject would
7   fit with ours. Uh ... and as I said, we are a rather heavily
8   booked church ... why just this week alone ... let's see
9   here ... Monday — we have softball practice in the
10   afternoon for the high schoolers, and in the evening,
11   Sarah Plimpton will be showing her slides on wildlife. And
12   then Tuesday's out. *(Looks at calendar.)* Oh, my! *(Laughs)*
13   The senior citizens will be going roller skating. *(Laughs)*
14   Oh, and they do have a grand time! *(More laughs)* And then
15   Wednesday ... yes, we have the craft class and the men's
16   prayer breakfast ... uh-oh, no, that's been cancelled. Well
17   as you can see, we just don't have a thing ... but listen,
18   why don't you have your representative give us a contact
19   later in the fall ... *(Vocal "ooo's" start again as if Jesus is*
20   *exiting)* maybe something will have opened up, sir. Sir ...
21   *(Blackout)*
22
23
24
25
26
27
28
29
30
31
32
33
34
35

EIGHTEEN

The Pastoral Selection Committee

THE PASTORAL SELECTION COMMITTEE

The Pastoral Selection Committee visits a committee of people who are struggling with the issue of "who should be our new pastor?" Unfortunately, self-defined qualifications not-so-subtly enter into the discussion.

SCENE: This scene takes place in a room where the pastoral selection committee is meeting.

CHARACTERS: RON is a well-meaning mediator.
              BEV is a rather well-to-do, pseudo-spiritual type whose values are revealed in her prayers.
              JEANNIE is an equally dogmatic woman who defends her side to the end.

STAGING: At least five people should be in this sketch, even though only three have lines. They are seated in a small, open semicircle, facing the audience.

PROPS: Play with this one — whatever you feel is appropriate.

LIGHTING: Normal, with a blackout at the end.

1 RON: Well, I think you all know why I've called this special
2   meeting of the pastoral selection committee. We've
3   narrowed the possibilities down to two — both of them
4   very fine Christian men — and I thought we should get
5   together and pray for guidance before we make our final
6   recommendation to the congregation. *(General murmurs*
7   *of assent)* Our first possibility is one Mrs. Rogers suggested
8   *(Refers to notes)* of the, uh, Rev. Walter Fleishman,
9   presently serving at the Coral Gables Community
10   Church. *(BEV smiles as JEANNIE looks aloof.)* And the
11   other, which Mrs. Jones suggested, is Pastor Harry
12   Weltenschaung of the Lindfern Ave. Church in
13   Pittsburgh. *(JEANNIE beams, BEV looks cold. Pause.)* So
14   without further ado, I move we pray.
15 BEV: Second.
16 RON: It having been moved and seconded that we pray,
17   those in favor say, "Aye."
18 ALL: Aye.
19 RON: Opposed? *(Silence)* The "Ayes" have it. Let us pray.
20   *(They all bow their heads. There is an awkward pause. Finally*
21   *BEV and JEANNIE both start at once. They both stop, miming*
22   *graciously for the other to go first. BEV finally starts.)*
23 BEV: Our Father, thou knowest our need. Thou knowest we
24   have been without a pastor for nearly a year now, ever
25   since our beloved Dr. Chrysler had to go to Arizona for
26   his health. Thou knowest we need the right person to
27   lead our congregation. We know that thou knowest
28   already who wouldst be thy chosen servant to this task.
29   We pray that thou wouldst give us openness to thy choice.
30   We call to mind that the Rev. Fleishman of Coral Gables
31   was man of the year for 1991. We call to mind the fact
32   that the membership of Coral Gables' church tripled in
33   the two years of Rev. Fleishman's leadership. We call to
34   mind his lovely wife, Eloise, who we remember is an
35   accomplished pianist and chalk-talk artist. Most of all we

1   pray that none of us will put our own will above yours —
2   thine. Amen. *(Pause. JEANNIE clears her throat.)*
3 JEANNIE: Lord, as we come before you for guidance in this
4   important decision, we would not put our own personal
5   desires before thy perfect will. Keep us from seeing men
6   as the world would see them, judging by worldly success
7   and the applause of men. Help us to remember that the
8   Lord looks with favor on the humble, and help us to
9   remember as well, the 25,000 a year we'll have to dish
10   out to get this turkey in our church.
11 BEV: *(Cutting in)* We recall, oh Lord, your word that the
12   laborer is worthy of his hire.
13 JEANNIE: *(Cutting in higher)* We remember as well, oh Lord,
14   that we were 4,000 dollars in the hole last year and that
15   Rev. Weltenschaung will come to us for no more than
16   10,000 a year.
17 BEV: *(BEV turns on JEANNIE.)* Because that's all he's worth!
18 JEANNIE: Oh, is that so? Well, let me tell you, Mrs. Rogers . . .
19   just because he doesn't have any chalk-talking wife! *(Both
20   have risen, shouting at once. RON and the others rise, trying to*
21   *separate them as the lights fade to dim or possibly fade out into*
22   *chorus of "They'll Know We Are Christians by Our Love.")*
23   *(Blackout)*
24
25
26
27
28
29
30
31
32
33
34
35

NINETEEN

Choir Director

CHOIR DIRECTOR

A sketch about a choir member who disagrees with the musical taste of the director.

SCENE: This sketch takes place immediately after a Sunday morning worship session.

CHARACTERS: MR. SMITH, the choir director, is a rather domineering, somewhat haughty individual who runs his church music program with an iron hand.
MISS HOFFMAN is a middle-aged woman that might best be described as a "busybody" and who has strong personal opinions of her own.
Play both characters rather broadly to curb the sarcastic edge of the conversation.

STAGING: Action all takes place Centerstage with two microphones in that position. MR. SMITH is thanking people and saying goodbye as they leave.

PROPS: If your church choir director wears a robe, try and procure a robe. You might also want to have MISS HOFFMAN wear a hat.

LIGHTING: Normal with a blackout at the end.

1   *SETTING:*   Scene takes place immediately after Sunday morning
2   worship service. MR. SMITH, the choir director, is thanking
3   people and saying goodbye as they leave. MISS HOFFMAN will
4   soon enter.
5   **MR. SMITH:**   **Thank you very much . . . bye now. Thanks . . .**
6   **Thank you, hope you enjoyed the musical part of the**
7   **service this morning.** *(MISS HOFFMAN moves into the scene*
8   *warbling MR. SMITH's name in the distance.)*
9   **MISS HOFFMAN:**   **Mr. Smith . . . Oh, Mr. Smiiiith.** *(Arrives next*
10   *to him.)* **Excuse me, Mr. Smith, I was hoping maybe we**
11   **could slip away for a moment and —**
12   **MR. SMITH:**   *(Obviously not interested in whatever it is she has to*
13   *say and trying to put her off. Looks toward someone leaving.)*
14   **Nice job on that solo this morning! Remember, we're**
15   **counting on you again next week. Take care of that voice**
16   **now. Bye-bye.**
17   **MISS HOFFMAN:**   **Mr. Smith!**
18   **MR. SMITH:**   *(Perturbed)* **Yes, Miss Hoffman.**
19   **MISS HOFFMAN:**   **Well, it's about the music we've been**
20   **singing over the past few months . . . since you've been**
21   **with us.**
22   **MR. SMITH:**   **Oh, it has been exciting, hasn't it?**
23   **Brahms . . . Handel . . . Bach. And how about the chorale**
24   **this morning? Wasn't that simply wonderful?**
25   **MISS HOFFMAN:**   **Well, as your organist, I did find a few of**
26   **the pedal sections just a little trying.** *(Laughs nervously.)*
27   **MR. SMITH:**   **Yes, I did notice a few, rather obvious mistakes.**
28   **Perhaps a little more practice would be in order.**
29   **MISS HOFFMAN:**   **Well, I did spend a good deal of time on**
30   **that number last week.**
31   **MR. SMITH:**   **Well, you know what they say, Miss Hoffman,**
32   **"Practice makes perfect."** *(They both tokenly laugh.)*
33   **MISS HOFFMAN:**   *(Laughter quickly dies into her line.)*
34   **Yes . . . well, Mr. Smith, what I wanted to talk to you about**
35   **was that I don't feel you fully understand the musical**

1   traditions of our church.

2   MR. SMITH: Oh, really, Miss Hoffman?

3   MISS HOFFMAN: Well, our people have grown to love the
4   more heart-warming forms of gospel songs and hymns.
5   Now, I for one have been greatly blessed by the hymns of
6   Fanny Crosby. And Mr. Smith, in the last two months,
7   you've not sung one Fanny Crosby.

8   MR. SMITH: Fanny . . . Crosby?

9   MISS HOFFMAN: Oh yes, there are so many . . .

10   MR. SMITH: Fanny Crosby, Miss Hoffman?

11   MISS HOFFMAN: Uh . . . yes.

12   MR. SMITH: Daughter of . . . Bing Crosby?

13   MISS HOFFMAN: *(A bit disgusted)* Mr. Smith . . . I don't
14   believe we're communicating. *(Pauses)* What I'm trying to
15   say is that . . . well, I've received quite a few comments as
16   of late about some of the hymns and anthems you've been
17   using and . . . well, I don't know how to put this but . . .
18   frankly . . . it's just that they all sound so . . . Roman
19   Catholic.

20   MR. SMITH: *(Starting to get mad)* Now, Miss Hoffman, I am
21   making a serious effort to educate the musical taste of this
22   congregation.

23   MISS HOFFMAN: But, the "Hallelujah Chorus" for the infant
24   choir?

25   MR. SMITH: *(Smiling proudly)* Ah, yes. Well, I always say you
26   can't start training them too early in the finer things.

27   MISS HOFFMAN: Well, that may be . . . but we did so love to
28   hear their little voices on *(She begins singing very out of key.)*
29   "Climb, climb up sunshine mountain!" Oh, it was so
30   cute . . . all of them lifting up their hands together for the
31   motions. That's heart-warming. *(Pauses)* They can't do
32   hand motions to the "Hallelujah Chorus."

33   MR. SMITH: *(Extremely perturbed)* Now look, Miss Hoffman, I
34   have just completed four years of study at the Peabody
35   Institute of Music, with honors, I might add. I also directed

1   the men's glee club at the State University for two years
2   and led the Golden Valley Community Choir while I was
3   still in high school. You see, Miss Hoffman, I know my
4   music . . . so don't throw this Fanny, what's-her-face at me!
5 MISS HOFFMAN: Well, Mr. Sm . . .
6 MR. SMITH: And furthermore, I was hired by this church to
7   be its music director and therefore I feel that the music I
8   select is, in essence, selected by the Lord.
9 MISS HOFFMAN: Well, I don't mean to be sacrilegious, but
10   the "Lord" certainly does have poor taste.
11 MR. SMITH: The fact remains, Miss Hoffman, this is my choir.
12 MISS HOFFMAN: *(Frustrated and talking louder)* Well, that
13   certainly isn't a very helpful attitude. After all . . . we are
14   Christians!
15 MR. SMITH: Christians? That has absolutely nothing to do
16   with it.
17 MISS HOFFMAN: Very well, Mr. Smith. Either we bring back
18   Fanny Crosby, or perhaps you better begin praying that
19   the Lord will give you another organist.
20 MR. SMITH: *(Looks at the audience, acknowledging she has set
21   herself up. He calmly replies:)* Miss Hoffman, let me be frank.
22   Talent like yours, and I use the term loosely, might best
23   be suited for a roller skating rink. Have you ever
24   considered ministering there?
25 MISS HOFFMAN: *(Very mad)* Well, if that's your attitude, let
26   me remind you that if I go, the infant choir goes . . . the
27   piano in the Junior department goes, the music library
28   goes and . . . and, let's not forget that painting of Jesus in
29   the ladies' lounge. That's mine, too, you know. The ladies
30   of this church will not take kindly to losing their painting.
31 MR. SMITH: Now Miss Hoffman, let's be reasonable
32   . . . *(Conversation breaks into an argument as the first line of*
33   *"They'll Know We Are Christians by Our Love" is sung.*
34   *Blackout.)*
35

TWENTY

Karen's Choice

KAREN'S CHOICE

What do you do if you end up pregnant and you're not married? This sketch looks at the feelings and choices that go with that issue.

SCENE: This sketch takes place on opposite ends of the stage.

CHARACTERS: BRET is a patient, understanding friend. He's in his early to middle thirties.
KAREN is 32 and at this point is very troubled about the choices in front of her.

STAGING: The scene is done on opposite sides of the stage.

PROPS: There should be chairs on both sides of the stage, and two telephones.

LIGHTING: Normal with a slow fade at the end.

1   **SETTING:**   Scene begins in darkness with a phone ringing. As soon
2   as BRET answers the phone, the lights come up on the players.
3   BRET: *(Yawning)* **Hello.**
4   KAREN: **Hello, Bret, it's me.**
5   BRET: *(Still asleep)* **Oh . . . good . . . me who?**
6   KAREN: **Karen. Did I get you out of bed?**
7   BRET: *(Sleepy)* **No . . . I've been up for hours. Karen who?**
8   KAREN: **Martin.**
9   BRET: *(Waking up)* **Oh, Karen . . . Wow, it's been a long time.**
10   **How are you, married lady?**
11   KAREN: **Single.**
12   BRET: **Huh? I thought you got married.** *(He listens for a response*
13   *from her.)* **Karen? Are you all right?**
14   KAREN: **I need some advice.**
15   BRET: **Oh, no . . . this is where I always get in trouble.**
16   KAREN: **You're the only person I feel I can trust. Please?**
17   BRET: **OK.**
18   KAREN: *(Long pause)* **This is difficult. I'm scared.**
19   BRET: **It's OK . . . I'm with you.**
20   KAREN: *(Reluctantly)* **I'm going to have a baby.**
21   BRET: *(Excited)* **That's great!** *(Pause)* **Isn't it?**
22   KAREN: **This wasn't supposed to happen! It wasn't supposed**
23   **to work out like this! What am I going to do?**
24   BRET: *(Taken aback)* **Uh . . . have you told . . .**
25   KAREN: **Yes, I told him last night.**
26   BRET: **And . . .**
27   KAREN: **And he said he didn't want a kid. I feel so stupid,**
28   **Bret. I can't have this baby! I can't afford to raise a child**
29   **alone. How will I ever tell my family?**
30   BRET: **They'll understand . . .**
31   KAREN: **I don't know . . .**
32   BRET: **Sure they will. You've got to tell them.** *(No response)*
33   **Karen?**
34   KAREN: **Yeah?**
35   BRET: **You're going to tell them, right?**

1   KAREN: I haven't decided.

2   BRET: It's going to be a little difficult to keep them from

3   noticing a child around the house, don't you think?

4   KAREN: Bret, I'm 32. I've had some health problems. The

5   doctor said I could never have children.

6   BRET: Doctors can be wrong. Only God knows those things

7   for sure.

8   KAREN: I can't raise this child. I have no money . . .

9   BRET: Don't you think God can provide that?

10   KAREN: I don't know what to think.

11   BRET: Look, you're going to have a baby. A tiny baby. You'll

12   be a great mother. You'll learn to deal with the financial

13   thing.

14   KAREN: I just can't see myself with a child. I can't see myself

15   with a child. I can't have the baby.

16   BRET: There isn't any other option.

17   KAREN: *(Long pause)* Yes, there is.

18   BRET: *(Realizing what she is thinking)* Karen?

19   KAREN: This is the 90's, Bret. I have a choice.

20   BRET: What about the baby? Karen . . . I can't tell you what

21   to do. I just don't want you to do something that you'll

22   regret for the rest of your life.

23   KAREN: You're too late.

24   BRET: I know this isn't easy, but something good can come

25   out of something bad. Look, I'll help in any way I can.

26   Let's go talk to your parents, OK?

27   KAREN: What . . . and say their old maid daughter is going

28   to have their grandchild?

29   BRET: No, that their daughter, whom they love very much,

30   is going to have their grandchild.

31   KAREN: I don't know . . .

32   BRET: It'll be all right. Trust me.

33   KAREN: That's hard. The last man that said that to me just

34   walked out.

35   BRET: I won't. Neither will the Lord.

1   **KAREN:**   I need time to think. *(Pause)* **Thanks. I'll call back,**
2   **OK?**
3   **BRET:**   **I'll be waiting.** *(Lights fade.)*
4
5
6
7
8
9
10
11
12
13
14
15
16
17
18
19
20
21
22
23
24
25
26
27
28
29
30
31
32
33
34
35

TWENTY-ONE

Too Much Complaining

TOO MUCH COMPLAINING

A sketch that deals with the pressures of working in a church and asks the question, "Is it worth it?"

SCENE: The scene takes place in a pastor's office.

CHARACTERS: BECKY is a very efficient and very frustrated church secretary.
PASTOR is a very calm and patient individual.

STAGING: The scene should be done Centerstage, dressed to look like a pastor's office.

PROPS: Ideally, the scene should have a desk with a couple of chairs in front of it. For added interest, set up a punching bag in the office.

LIGHTING: Normal with a quick blackout at the end.

1   BECKY: *(Bursting through the door)* **That's it! That's it! I quit!**
2   **Just give me five minutes to write my resignation and an**
3   **hour to clean my desk, and I'm history! I'll leave a**
4   **forwarding address.** *(Starts to exit.)*
5   PASTOR: **Whoa, hold it! Why are you so upset?**
6   BECKY: **Upset? Who is upset? I'm not upset! I'm livid!**
7   PASTOR: **Why are you livid?**
8   BECKY: **Why, you ask? Where were you last night?**
9   PASTOR: **I was here at the leadership board meeting . . . with**
10   **you.**
11   BECKY: **And you ask why I'm livid?**
12   PASTOR: *(Getting up from behind his desk, moving towards her.)*
13   **So it has to do with that?**
14   BECKY: **Of course it has to do with that!**
15   PASTOR: **Have a seat.**
16   BECKY: **I don't want a seat. I want a gun. I want to solve the**
17   **overcrowding problem in our sanctuary every Sunday**
18   **morning.**
19   PASTOR: **Come on, Becky . . . . Sit down, and let's talk.**
20   BECKY: **I don't want to talk . . . I want to quit. You can find**
21   **me at the McDonalds on Peak. I'll be the little fat girl**
22   **making fries.** *(Starts to exit, then turns.)* **Who do they think**
23   **they are?**
24   PASTOR: **Who?**
25   BECKY: **Oh, you know, all those pea brains that showed up**
26   **last night to complain about everything. You know,**
27   **complain about the parking, complain about the carpet,**
28   **complain about the music. Why, Bernie Davies,**
29   **complaining about the songs we sing. What does he**
30   **care . . . he can't sing. My terrier carries a better tune. And**
31   **Mildred Ward . . . if she says to me one more time that the**
32   **choir needs to wear robes, I'll personally stick the entire**
33   **closetful up her nose. And the scary thing is . . . it would**
34   **fit! I've had it! I thought I had a calling from God to be in**
35   **church ministry . . . but I must have been overhearing**

1   someone else's conversation. Goodbye!

2 PASTOR: Becky, let's talk.

3 BECKY: About what? And why are you so calm? Did you hear

4   what they said about your sermon?

5 PASTOR: Yes, that it was too personal and negative.

6 BECKY: Well?

7 PASTOR: Well what?

8 BECKY: Well ... don't you wanna punch their lights

9   out ... call fire down from heaven ... sic a couple of angry

10   angels on them?

11 PASTOR: Now that's an interesting concept.

12 BECKY: Yeah, well, I've got a couple more where that came

13   from. I mean, all they do is gripe. We try to come up with

14   services that minister to the whole body and what do they

15   do? Complain! I've had it up to here. *(Motioning to her neck)*

16   I'm gonna become a nun, lock myself in a convent, and

17   transcribe old documents ... that is, after I finish a box of

18   chocolates to calm my nerves.

19 PASTOR: Look, nobody said ministry was going to be easy.

20 BECKY: I'm not looking for easy. I'd settle for mildly

21   bearable. If Jesus had those people on the riverbank

22   waiting for him, he would've kept walking on the

23   water ... in the other direction! They would have said the

24   sermon on the mount was too personal and negative. I

25   mean, why should he care? Why should I care?

26 PASTOR: I don't know ... but he does, and we should try.

27 BECKY: I'm finished trying. There comes a point when it just

28   becomes too much.

29 PASTOR: Well, only you can decide that.

30 BECKY: That's it? You're not gonna soothe my ruffled

31   feathers and expound profound words of wisdom that will

32   lead me in the way of righteousness? *(He smiles at her.)*

33   Well, then, what are you good for?

34 PASTOR: Not much. Maybe a listening ear. Maybe an

35   occasional good sermon that might make a small

1   difference in someone's life. Maybe I'm just a quasi-
2   consistent person that can dedicate (baptize) a baby or
3   bury the dead. *(Pause)* I'm not going to tell you anything
4   will change. People are going to complain, no matter what
5   we do. So, let's keep plugging away, doing what we believe
6   in, hoping and praying that somewhere along the way, it
7   will make a difference in God's kingdom. That's all God
8   asks.
9 BECKY: For being a "quasi-consistent" person, you're pretty
10   smart. You get a little personal though . . . and I think you
11   could be more positive.
12 PASTOR: I'll work on it. *(Idea)* Tell you what . . . I'll buy you
13   lunch.
14 BECKY: Great! Where are we going?
15 PASTOR: McDonalds. *(Blackout)*
16
17
18
19
20
21
22
23
24
25
26
27
28
29
30
31
32
33
34
35

TWENTY-TWO

Invitation at Dinner

INVITATION AT DINNER
by PHIL LOLLAR

Can going to church really help a marriage that is on the rocks?

SCENE: This sketch takes place in a restaurant
                 at lunch time.

CHARACTERS: PAUL is the thirty-something friend of
                 DAVE. He is impatient and obviously on
                 edge about something.
                 DAVE is his faithful and honest best
                 friend.

STAGING: Should be done Centerstage around a
                 table.

PROPS: Use whatever you like to give the impres-
                 sion of a restaurant. Sound effects might
                 be nice.

LIGHTING: Normal with a blackout at the end.

1   PAUL: *(Calling out)* **Waiter? Waiter!** *(An impatient sigh)*
2   **Great . . .**
3   DAVE: **He's kinda busy — he'll get to us.**
4   PAUL: **Why do we keep coming here? If I wanted terrible**
5   **food and lousy service, I'd go home for lunch. I can get it**
6   **there for free . . .** *(Uncomfortable long pause . . . PAUL looks*
7   *at DAVE)* **Sorry . . .**
8   DAVE: **Are you telling me things aren't good at home or is it**
9   **that you're not getting enough bulk in your diet?**
10 PAUL: **Both.**
11 DAVE: **Anything I can do?**
12 PAUL: **I don't think there's anything anybody can do. We've**
13   **tried everything. I just don't know what the problem is . . .**
14 DAVE: **Maybe you're trying too hard. You know, sometimes**
15   **we want complex answers to a problem when the answer**
16   **is really very simple. It's like this story I heard a couple**
17   **of days ago. This guy had a dog that developed a rash on**
18   **its tummy. It'd itch so bad that the only way the dog could**
19   **get relief was to crawl along on the St. Augustine grass in**
20   **the front yard. Well, the guy tried everything to get rid of**
21   **the rash, and nothing worked. So he finally took the dog**
22   **to the vet. The vet ran some tests, then came back out and**
23   **said, "We know what's wrong with the dog." The man said,**
24   **"What is it?" The vet said, "He has an allergy — he is**
25   **allergic to St. Augustine grass."** *(They laugh.)*
26 PAUL: **Not bad!**
27 DAVE: **I stole it from our pastor.**
28 PAUL: **Really?**
29 DAVE: **Yeah, he's always coming up with jokes like that. You**
30   **oughta come to church and hear him sometime. I think**
31   **you'd enjoy it.**
32 PAUL: **I don't know. I've never been into that church stuff.**
33   **Sounds boring.**
34 DAVE: **Not Pastor Keller.**
35 PAUL: **No offense, Dave, but you've never impressed me as**

1   the "church type."

2 DAVE: Didn't used to be, that's for sure. In fact, there was a

3   time when you wouldn't have caught me dead in church.

4 PAUL: Why the change?

5 DAVE: A lot of things. For one, I woke up one morning and

6   realized that I'd had it with the "yuppie rat race." There's

7   more to life than a home and a BMW, you know?

8 PAUL: You're sounding like a radio psychologist.

9 DAVE: Sorry. But really, Paul . . . When I'm on my deathbed,

10   how much comfort am I gonna get from all the things I

11   own? Is my Rolex watch gonna say I love you? No . . . the

12   only ones who'll say that will be my family. And I almost

13   lost them.

14 PAUL: What? Wait a minute! You didn't tell me about this!

15 DAVE: I didn't tell anybody. You see, I came home from work

16   and found Ellen all packed and walking out the door.

17 PAUL: Why?

18 DAVE: A lot of reasons. She said she couldn't take it anymore.

19 PAUL: Sounds familiar . . .

20 DAVE: And I, typical male that I am, didn't even see it coming.

21 PAUL: What did you do?

22 DAVE: The usual. "The Dance of Excuses." You know, "If

23   only you'd do this!" and "Why can't you understand that!"

24   Or, "You knew what I was when you married me!"

25 PAUL: *(Smiles)* Oh, yeah — I've heard that one a few times . . .

26 DAVE: Finally, though, when we got tired of sparring, we

27   realized that we didn't have any grounding. We were just

28   living for things, you know, to get ahead. Oh, we both said

29   we loved each other, but that doesn't mean a whole lot

30   when you don't know what love is.

31 PAUL: And you found that at church?

32 DAVE: As crazy as it sounds, we did. Just like the guy with

33   the dog, we were looking for a complex solution when the

34   simple answer was right in front of us. It's all there in the

35   Bible, Paul. It's not just a lot of "pie in the sky" stuff, either.

1   It's a collection of real, solid guidelines.

2   PAUL: I — I just don't know, Dave. My marriage may be too

3   far gone for the Bible and church to salvage . . .

4   DAVE: Maybe . . . but is it getting any better by not coming?

5   *(Pause)*

6   PAUL: You know, you're a very persuasive man.

7   DAVE: *(Embarrassed)* Oh, I don't know . . .

8   PAUL: Oh, you are.

9   DAVE: Well, if you say so.

10   PAUL: So do you think you might be able to persuade the

11   waiter to come over here and take our order?

12   DAVE: *(Laughs)* I'll see what I can do . . . *(They continue to laugh*

13   *and the lights fade to blackout.)*

14

15

16

17

18

19

20

21

22

23

24

25

26

27

28

29

30

31

32

33

34

35

TWENTY-THREE

Sure You Won't Change Your Mind?

SURE YOU WON'T CHANGE YOUR MIND?
by JIM CUSTER

A sketch that looks at the possible cost of commitment.

SCENE: This sketch takes place in a comfortable but sterile room.

CHARACTERS: JENNY: A sweet, mildly attractive nurse.
                   JACK: A normal, middle aged man full of conviction.
                   DAN: A lawyer friend who does his best to talk sense into Jack.
                   MAN #1 and MAN #2: Tall, obviously strong men in a subtle type of uniform.

STAGING: Scene should be done Centerstage. Set should resemble a spartan but comfortable living room. If possible, a window and door would be effective.

PROPS: A blood pressure checking device
                   Stethoscope
                   Assorted legal-looking papers and pen

LIGHTING: Normal: light comes up when dialogue starts; blackout at the end.

1 **SETTING:** *JACK is sitting in a chair in a small but comfortable*
2   *room.*
3 **JENNY:** *(Entering)* **OK, Mr. Wilson, we have to check your**
4   **blood pressure. Just roll up your sleeve.** *(He does.)* **Isn't it**
5   **an absolutely lovely day?**
6 **JACK: I . . . I haven't been outside today.**
7 **JENNY: Oh, of course you haven't. Silly me. Oh well . . . it is**
8   **an absolutely lovely day. The birds are singing . . . the**
9   **wind is lifting across the hills.**
10 **JACK: Very poetic.**
11 **JENNY: Well, it is a very poetic day.** *(Listens to his heartbeat.)*
12   **You're ticking away. Tic, tic, tic . . . You definitely have a**
13   **strong heart. You must be an athlete.**
14 **JACK: A little racquetball.**
15 **JENNY: Well, everyone should have a heart like you. So what**
16   **was for dinner? It's very important, you know.**
17 **JACK: I told them I didn't want dinner.**
18 **JENNY: You didn't want any? The sky's the limit, you know.**
19   **You should've ordered big. If I had my wish . . . it would**
20   **be steak and lobster. I love to dip it in butter. You know,**
21   **and have a little baked potato on the side.**
22 **JACK: Definitely sounds good.**
23 **JENNY: You know, Mr. Wilson . . . it's not too late to change**
24   **your mind about this. A lot of people have. It saves a lot**
25   **of unpleasantness. Why, you could be out enjoying the**
26   **day,** *(Nudges him.)* **playing a little racquetball, maybe**
27   **writing some poetry. I think it's worth considering.**
28 **JACK: It's not possible.**
29 **JENNY: Oh, sure it is. But you know what they say, "Your**
30   **ship won't come in 'til you row out to meet it."**
31 **JACK: Well, whoever "they" are . . . they don't understand.**
32   **The sea isn't always calm enough for rowing.**
33 **JENNY: Huh? Men. You're all very stubborn. Not that it will**
34   **keep me from liking you, but . . . .** *(Enter DAN)*
35 **DAN: Hey, big guy.** *(Shakes his hand.)*

1   JACK: I can't speak for Wendell . . . only me.
2   DAN: How 'bout Pastor Adkinson?
3   JACK: How about Pastor Adkinson?
4   DAN: What I'm saying is . . . he's a Pastor. If anyone should
5   know what's right, it's him.
6   JACK: Dan. I've thought about this . . . I looked at the cost.
7   I've made my decision . . . not because I have to, but
8   because I want to. I know that's hard for you to see, but . . .
9   DAN: OK, OK . . . You don't have to convince me. I just
10   thought I'd say something. *(Pulls out papers.)* I need you to
11   sign some papers. It keeps things all neat and tidy. Just
12   read through it and sign on the X's.
13   JACK: *(Reads briefly.)* Looks fine to me. Got a pen?
14   DAN: Oh yeah . . . . I guess you'll need one.
15   JACK: Unless you want me to write it in blood. *(They look at*
16   *each other. JACK signs.)* Well, that's that. *(Knock on the door)*
17   DAN: You're sure?
18   JACK: I'm sure. *(In walk JENNY and two men dressed in*
19   *uniforms.)*
20   MAN #1:   Mr. Jack Wilson?
21   JACK: Yes.
22   MAN #1:   It's time.
23   JACK: I'm ready.
24   MAN #1:   I am instructed to give you one final chance . . . will
25   you renounce your faith in Jesus Christ and take your
26   personal identification number?
27   JACK: *(Long pause, looks around, then speaks slowly.)* No, sir.
28   MAN #1:   Very well, then. Follow me. *(He turns and exits.)*
29   DAN: No changing your mind?
30   JACK: No . . . *(Smiles)* No changing my heart.
31
32
33
34
35

TWENTY-FOUR

Prayer Is Not an Option

PRAYER IS NOT AN OPTION
by DONNA SHERON

This sketch finds students questioning their teacher's rule of "no prayer in school."

SCENE: A sixth grade classroom, present time.

CHARACTERS: MRS. SHNYDER, Voice of the PRINCI-
                PAL, SAM, SUSAN, CHRISTY,
                JOHNNY, MARYANN, PAM, (Children
                can either be played by children, or played
                by adults acting as children).

STAGING: Small desks are Stage Right; a black
                board up Center Stage. The teacher's desk
                is Stage Left.

PROPS: Tuba
                Apple
                Paper airplanes, lunch boxes, assorted
                school supplies

LIGHTING: Normal with a blackout at the end.

1   *SETTING:*   *The school bell rings. JOHNNY enters, holding his tuba,*
2   *and gives the teacher an apple. The CHILDREN rush in noisily*
3   *and take their seats. MRS. SHNYDER is at her desk. The*
4   *CHILDREN are throwing airplanes, trading lunches, etc.*
5   MRS. SHNYDER: Class . . . settle down. *(They simmer down to*
6   *a murmur.)* Everyone please stand to salute the flag. *(The*
7   *CHILDREN stand and say the Pledge of Allegiance. Some giggle*
8   *through it, others forget the words but "with liberty and justice*
9   *for all" should be heard very clearly.)*
10   CHILDREN: Ugh!!, Gross! *(Etc.)*
11   VOICE OF PRINCIPAL: Oh, yes! I almost forgot. I received
12   a very important bulletin from the Federal Government.
13   An official notice has been sent out to all the public schools
14   in the United States. It reads, "The bill concerning prayer
15   in public schools has not been passed." I repeat, NOT been
16   passed. Which means it is ILLEGAL to pray during school
17   hours — this includes silent prayer, as well as verbal
18   prayer. Please, teachers, this must be enforced — anyone
19   caught breaking this rule will be dealt with severely. Have
20   a great day!
21   MRS. SHNYDER: Did everyone understand that? He means
22   ABSOLUTELY, POSITIVELY, NO praying. So . . . I don't
23   want to see anyone even *looking* as if they're in prayer.
24   No bowing of heads, *no* closing of eyes. It is no longer an
25   option. There is *(Writing on blackboard)* NO PRAYING IN
26   SCHOOL. Does anyone have any questions?
27   SUSAN: *(Raising hand)* What about at recess? Or at lunch?
28   MRS. SHNYDER: No. Not from the time you get to school
29   until the time you go home.
30   JOHNNY: Can we still pray at home? I mean, my family says
31   grace — are we breaking the law? Will we go to jail?
32   MRS. SHNYDER: No! Of course not! It's just that I believe
33   our government doesn't want us influencing your
34   thinking — forcing any ideas into your young minds.
35   CHILDREN: *(Wide-eyed)* Oh . . .

1   **MRS. SHNYDER:**   So, now it is against the law for us to pray,
2   or discuss God, the Bible, and so on in the classroom. We
3   don't want to break the law, do we?
4   **CHILDREN:**   *(Shaking their heads)* No . . .
5   **MRS. SHNYDER:**   OK, then. Since we are on the subject of
6   law, let us begin with our history lesson.
7   **CHILDREN:**   Boo! Grody to the max! *(Etc. Pulling out books and*
8   *paper noisily.)*
9   **MRS. SHNYDER:**   We were last discussing ancient history.
10   Athens' early democracy. *(Reading)* "In 508 B.C., the
11   Athenians adopted a new constitution which made the
12   state a democracy." Who can tell me what a democracy
13   is? *(CHRISTY raises her hand.)*
14   **MRS. SHNYDER:**   Yes, Christy . . .
15   **CHRISTY:**   Mrs. Shnyder, what does B.C. stand for?
16   **MRS. SHNYDER:**   Before Christ. *(Children all gasp, covering*
17   *their mouths.)*
18   **SAM:**   *(Whiny)* I'm telling . . .
19   **MRS. SHNYDER:**   *(Flustered)* That'll be quite enough. It's time
20   for a pop quiz on the United States Bill of Rights.
21   **CHILDREN:**   Oh, come on . . . I can't believe this. *(Etc.)*
22   **MARYANN:**   That's not fair! I didn't study!
23   **MRS. SHNYDER:** All right, young lady — you first.
24   *(CHILDREN laugh)* Please stand and recite the First
25   Amendment.
26   **MARYANN:**   *(Standing)* Uh . . . um . . . Congress shall make no
27   law re—specting, um . . . of our religion . . . Pro—hi—bit—
28   ing the free exercise of it . . . the freedom of speech,
29   or . . . or . . . the freedom of the press —
30   **JOHNNY:**   *(Jumping up)* Hey! The first amendment says
31   freedom of religion in it! Doesn't that mean the people are
32   free to choose?
33   **SUSAN:**   *(Standing)* Yeah, aren't we *free* to pray if we want?
34   **CHRISTY:**   It's in the Constitution!
35   **SAM:**   Yeah! Why don't they ask us if we *want* to pray? It's

1   our right! *(Climbing on the desk)* **LET ME SPEAK TO THE**
2   **PRESIDENT!!**
3   **MRS. SHNYDER:** *(Pulling him down)* **All right, wise guy — to**
4   **the blackboard — now! Write "I will not pray in school"**
5   **until I tell you to stop.** *(To the class)* **This is a serious**
6   **business. We are the most powerful nation in the world.**
7   **We CANNOT take what our government tells us lightly!**
8   **SCIENCE!** *(Becoming more nervous — flipping through her*
9   *textbooks.)* **Evolution ... Evolution means an orderly**
10   **development. We say that buds evolve into flowers. In most**
11   **scientific books, however, the word means organic**
12   **evolution, or the *theory* of evolution applied to living**
13   **things. This *theory* says that plants and animals have**
14   **changed through generation after generation and are still**
15   **changing today. This means that all things now living on**
16   **earth are much-changed descendants of others that lived**
17   **thousands — even millions — of years ago. Take humans,**
18   **for example. We are one of the species of vertebrate**
19   **animals. Most scientists hypothesize that since all**
20   **vertebrates have spines, and there are as many different**
21   **bone structures as there are species of vertebrate animals,**
22   **this proves that we all evolve from some common lower**
23   **ancestor — like the monkey, for example.**
24   **CHILDREN:** Ooh, neat.
25   **MARYANN:** What's a theory?
26   **MRS. SHNYDER:** Well, I'm not sure that this is the time ... oh,
27   very well. *(Picks up the dictionary.)* Webster says a theory
28   is: "An unproved assumption, ... an abstract
29   thought ... as speculation." Which means, children, that
30   science has used its knowledge to tell us how things
31   *probably* happened.
32   **CHRISTY:** But you said it *proved* we were from monkeys.
33   **MRS. SHNYDER:** Well, I didn't say that exactly ... but, since
34   so many creatures have the common vertebrae, as I was
35   saying, then science accepts this as evidence that ...

1   PAM: But couldn't that mean that God sorta created
2   everything like that?
3   SAM: My arm's getting tired. *(Still writing)*
4   MRS. SHNYDER: Ah ... but there's no proof whatsoever that
5   God ... *(Pause)* We shouldn't be discussing this.
6   SAM: Can I stop yet?
7   JOHNNY: My dad says that the Bible proves that God *did*
8   create everything.
9   MRS. SHNYDER: Now, let's not ...
10   MARYANN: Is the Bible as good as a theory?
11   SAM: My arm's gonna break!
12   MRS. SHNYDER: Let's all be quiet now ...
13   SUSAN: If God didn't create everything and we came from
14   monkeys, where'd the monkeys come from?
15   PAM: And what about worms? Did they evolve too?
16   JOHNNY: No, God *created* them.
17   MRS. SHNYDER: Quiet! If I hear one more syllable
18   concerning God, the Bible, or anything other than
19   textbook material — you will ALL be expelled. Do you
20   understand me? *(The CHILDREN are all seated like meek little*
21   *lambs.)* OK then ... let's change the subject — completely.
22   *(Calms down.)* On to our music lesson, then we'll recess for
23   lunch. Let's stand and sing, ah, *(Thinks)* "America the
24   Beautiful."
25   ALL: "Oh beautiful, for spacious skies, for amber waves of
26   grain. For purple mountain's majesty, above the fruited
27   plains. America, America." *(The CHILDREN stop singing —*
28   *MRS. SHNYDER continues alone.)*
29   MRS. SHNYDER: *(Singing)* "God rest his hand on thee ... "
30   *(Realizing what she's sung.)* Oh ... *(Exasperated, she exits.*
31   *Everyone sits quietly for a few moments.)*
32   SAM: *(Still writing)* Can I stop yet? *(Blackout)*
33
34
35

TWENTY-FIVE

Dinner

DINNER
by JIM CUSTER and BOB HOOSE

A one-minute discussion sketch that looks at one dinner in the life of one Christian family.

SCENE:	The sketch takes place in the dining room of an all-American family.
CHARACTERS:	MOM is someone who would like a quiet, peaceful, dinner with the whole family. DAD is caught just trying to "catch up." SIS is a young teenage girl who is hung up on what she eats. SON is in a rush, and "dinner at home" is not in the plans.
STAGING:	The scene should take place around a table with exits to both side of the stage.
PROPS:	Ideally, the sketch should be done with real food. However, it is not absolutely necessary. Silverware and plates should be used though.
LIGHTING:	Normal with a quick blackout at the end.

1   MOM: *(Yelling)* **Dinner's ready!**
2   SON: *(Entering)* **I gotta hurry ... youth group's going to a**
3   **concert. Can I just put something in a bag?**
4   MOM: **No. You can sit for ten minutes.**
5   SON: **That's the max, Mom.**
6   MOM: *(Yelling)* **Dinner's ready ... it's getting cold!**
7   SON: *(Yelling)* **Yeah! It's getting cold!**
8   MOM: *(To SON)* **Sit!**
9   DAD: *(Entering)* **What's all the yelling?**
10 MOM: **It's getting cold.**
11 SON: **And I have to leave.**
12 DAD: **Why?**
13 MOM: **Because food does that when it's left off the stove.**
14 DAD: **Huh?** *(Realizing she misunderstood)* **No, not the**
15   **food ... him.** *(Pointing at SON)* **Why does he have to leave?**
16 SIS: *(Entering)* **What's for dinner?**
17 MOM: **Pork chops.**
18 SIS: **I'll have a sandwich.**
19 SON: **Let's do it ... I have to run.**
20 MOM: *(To SIS)* **No sandwich. I fixed this ... you'll eat.** *(SON*
21   *makes the sound of a clock ticking.)*
22 DAD: **Don't tick at the table.**
23 SIS: *(To MOM)* **But it's pork.**
24 MOM: *(To SIS)* **So what? You're not Jewish.**
25 SON: *(Making the sound of a buzzer)* **Too late!** *(Starts to get up.)*
26 MOM: **But you haven't eaten.**
27 SON: **I'll take a roll.**
28 DAD: **We didn't pray.**
29 SON: *(Stops, looks up and holds up the roll.)* **Thanks, God.**
30 SIS: **But pork is unclean.**
31 MOM: **No, honey, I scrubbed it up just for you.**
32 DAD: *(Gets up to go after SON.)* **Hey! You still haven't told me**
33   **where you're going.** *(Exits)*
34 SIS: *(To MOM)* **They are cloven-footed animals.**
35 MOM: *(To DAD off stage)* **Wait!** *(To SIS)* **You're reading too**

1   much Old Testament, sweetheart.
2 SIS: I cannot partake. *(Exits)*
3 MOM: *(Sits at the table. Sighs.)* I just love these little family
4   times. *(Looks up.)* Well, Lord, it's just you and me. Want a
5   pork chop?
6
7
8
9
10
11
12
13
14
15
16
17
18
19
20
21
22
23
24
25
26
27
28
29
30
31
32
33
34
35

Jim Custer (left) and Bob Hoose

Custer & Hoose

Jim Custer has traveled with the **Jeremiah People** for fourteen years, delighting audiences nationwide and abroad with his wit and dramatic characters. He directed the group for eleven of those years. He has an extensive background in theatre, film, and radio, and has received national accolades for several Gospel Films and James Dobson productions.

Bob Hoose, producer for the **Jeremiah People**, has worked professionally with theatre, radio, and television for the last thirteen years. A talented musician, his credits range from Christian albums to the Civic Light Opera. In addition, he has implemented two successful drama ministries in Southern California.

Together, Jim and Bob have over thirty years of combined experience in Christian drama. They team up to present a dynamic two-man show, "Best of Friends," at churches nationwide, and also conduct seminars to aid churches in strengthening their drama ministries. They have a sketch for almost any occasion or topic within the church — hence, **The Best of the Jeremiah People**. They are currently working on their second two-man show which explores father relationships.